PROSPERO'S
BOOKS

PROSPERO'S BOOKS

A FILM OF SHAKESPEARE'S THE TEMPEST

BY PETER GREENAWAY

Four Walls Eight Windows, New York

Published by:

Four Walls Eight Windows
PO Box 548
Village Station
New York, N.Y., 10014

First edition.
First printing October 1991.
Published in association with Chatto & Windus.

Library of Congress Cataloging-in-Publication Data:

Greenaway, Peter.
Prospero's Books/by Peter Greenaway
—1st ed.
p.   cm.
Based on Shakespeare's *Tempest*.
I. Shakespeare, 1564-1615. Tempest.   II. Title.
PN1997.P777   1991   90-29878
791.43'72—dc20   CIP
ISBN: 0-941423-60-3

Color separation by Colorlito, Milan
Printed in Italy by New Interlitho

CONTENTS

PROSPERO'S ISLAND, REBUILT IN ALL IT'S MANY PARTS TO FIT THE REQUIREMENTS OF AN EXILED SCHOLAR FAR FROM HOME, DREAMING OF ITALY.

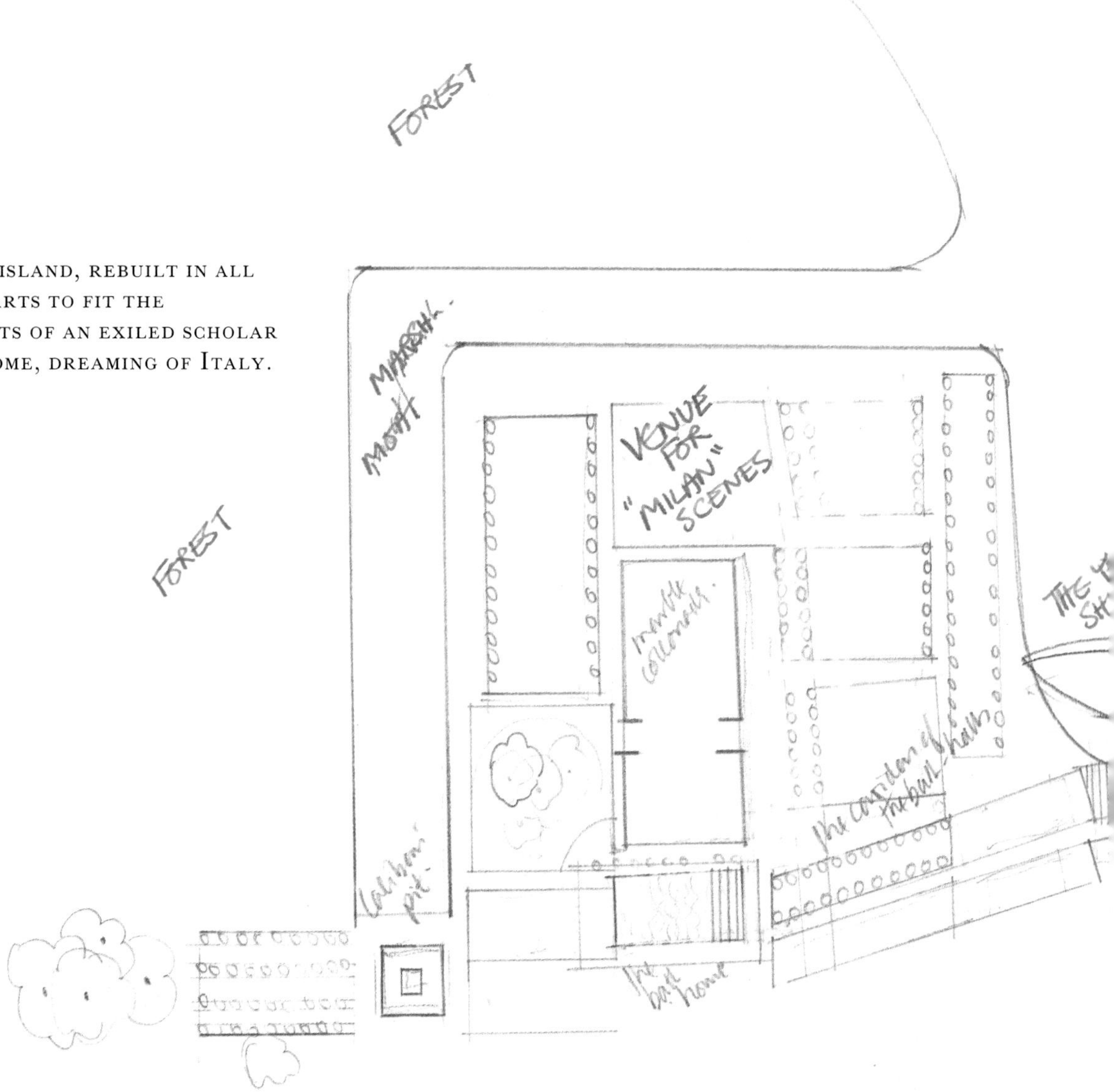

FOREST

FOREST

MARSH-MOAT

VENUE FOR "MILAN" SCENES

marble colonnade

Caliban's pit

the be-home

THE

The corridor of the mobile baths

ARIEL'S KNOTTY PINE

CALIBAN'S PIT.

THE BATH-HOUSE

THE BATH-HALLS

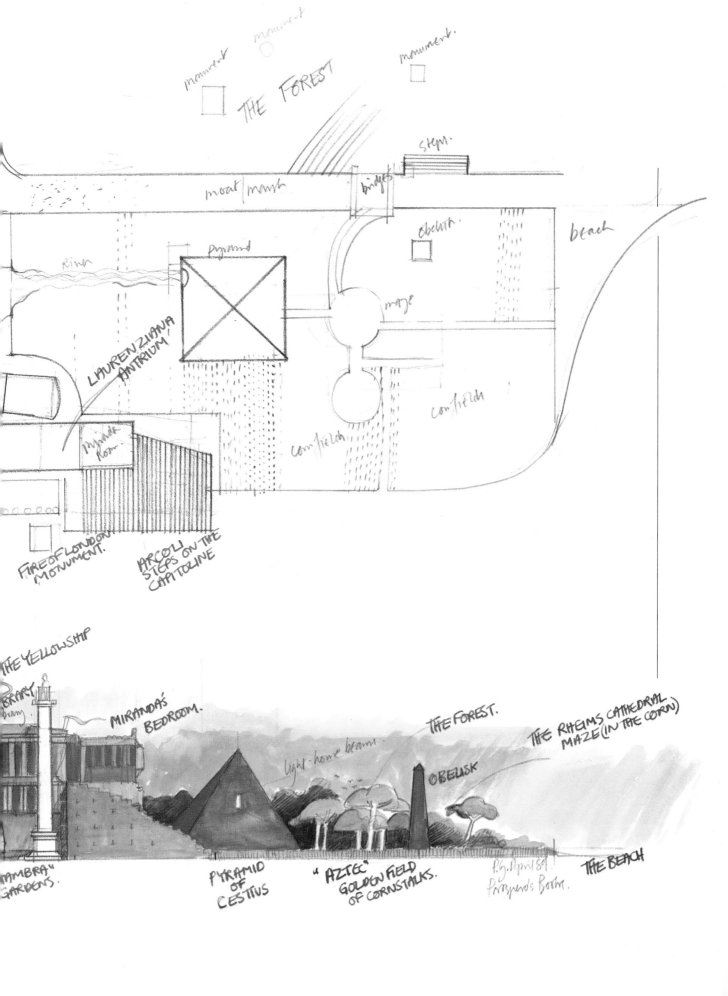

THE FOREST

monument   monument

monument.

steps.

moat/marsh   bridges

obelisk.

beach

River   Pyramid

LAURENZIANA
ANTRIUM

maze

cornfield

cornfield

Pyramid
Room

FIRE OF LONDON
MONUMENT.

MARCOLI
STEPS ON THE
CAPITOLINE

THE YELLOWSHIP
LIBRARY.

MIRANDA'S BEDROOM.

THE FOREST.

THE RHEIMS CATHEDRAL
MAZE (IN THE CORN)

Light-house beams

OBELISK

"ALHAMBRA"
GARDENS.

PYRAMID
OF
CESTIUS

"AZTEC"
GOLDEN FIELD
OF CORNSTALKS.

P.G. April 89
Prospero's Books.

THE BEACH

Knowing I lov'd my books,
he furnished me from mine
own library with volumes
that I (prize above my
Dukedom.

INTRODUCTION

The proposition to make a film of *The Tempest* came from Sir John Gielgud and this film-script was devised for his playing of Prospero.

Gielgud has played Prospero many times and has more than once considered committing the role to film. A particular wish of mine was to take maximum advantage of his powerful and authoritative ability to speak text – verse and prose – so that, as well as playing Prospero, he was persuaded to voice, for the most part, the dialogue of all the other characters in the drama as well.

The legitimacy for this approach is to see Prospero not just as the master manipulator of people and events but as their prime originator. On his island of exile, Prospero plans a drama to right the wrongs done to him. He invents characters to flesh out his imaginary fantasy to steer his enemies into his power, writes their dialogue, and having written it, he speaks the lines aloud, shaping the characters so powerfully through the words that they are conjured before us. The division between fact and fiction becomes indistinguishable; the characters walk and gesture, act and react, but still they do not speak. Their life-giving words are not their own, they continue to be the mouthpiece of Prospero, the master dramatist. And this is the way things remain for as long as *The Tempest* is guided by the traditions of the revenge tragedy. Then there is a twist, a rearrangement of events, a reversal. When his enemies are totally in his power, Prospero is admonished by Ariel for the ferocity of the revengeful humiliation he forces on them, and he repudiates his plans and turns instead to forgiveness. The characters that his passion for revenge had created out of words now speak for the first time with their own voices, brought to a full life by his act of compassion.

This strategy is made especially significant in a project that deliberately emphasises and celebrates the text as text, as the master material on which all the magic, illusion and deception of the play is based. Words making text, and text making

pages, and pages making books from which knowledge is fabricated in pictorial form – these are the persistently forefronted characteristics. As a consequence, and with good reason, we have called it *Prospero's Books*.

Prospero, omnipotent magician, inventor and manipulator of characters, can be conceivably appreciated as a Shakespearean self-portrait. Prospero is the last major role that Shakespeare invented, reputedly, in the last complete play he wrote, and there is much, both in the character and in the play, that can be understood as a leave-taking of the theatre and a farewell to role-playing and the manufacturing of illusion through words – not insignificant perhaps when Gielgud's seventy-year career on the stage is considered. In this script it is intended that there should be much deliberate cross-identification between Prospero, Shakespeare and Gielgud. At times they are indivisibly one person.

And the starting point for these strategies is Gonzalo's charity.

Knowing I loved my books, he furnished me
From mine own library with volumes that
I prize above my dukedom.

Gonzalo threw many books into the bottom of the leaky vessel that took Prospero out on to the sea away from Italy and Europe and into exile. Shakespeare does not, of course, elaborate what these volumes were. *Prospero's Books* speculates. There would need perhaps to be books on navigation and survival, there would need to be books for an elderly scholar to learn how to rear and educate a young daughter, how to colonise an island, farm it, subjugate its inhabitants, identify its plants and husband its wild beasts. There would need to be books to offer solace and advise patience and put past glory and present despondency into perspective. There would need to be books to encourage revenge. Twenty-four volumes might be enough to cover the information needed – bestiaries, a

11

herbal, cosmographies, atlases, astronomies, a book of languages, a book of utopias, a book of travellers' tales, a book of games. There may have been books whose immediate practical purpose was not fathomable – a pornography, a book of motion, a book of love, a book of colours and a book of 'Architecture and other Music'. In the event, all of the twenty-four volumes not only kept Prospero and Miranda alive, well and sane on their island but also made Prospero so powerful he could command the dead and make Neptune his servant. Against such magic, mortal enemies like the King of Naples could be considered small irritants.

Prospero's power is held in his relationship to his books, and *The Tempest* is witness to more than a few apparently conflicting facets of his personality – not all of them particularly praiseworthy. What was it, in those books, that made Prospero not only powerful but also a moralising scold and a petty revenger, a benevolent despot, a jealous father and also a master designer of song and dance? Are we truly the product of what we read?

After twelve years of exile, Prospero's island has become a place of illusion and deception whose references are forged by an unhappy scholar recreating a little Renaissance kingdom far from Europe. It is a place where the indigenous spirits are persuaded to impersonate classical mythological figures, where Prospero dresses like a Venetian doge, where Caliban dances and there are four Ariels to represent the elements, and the world is appreciated and referenced with the architecture, paintings and classical literature Prospero has imported. With such a fabric, it will be no surprise that it is an island full of superimposed images, of shifting mirrors and mirror-images – true mirages – where pictures conjured by text can be as tantalisingly substantial as objects and facts and events, constantly framed and re-framed. This framing and re-framing becomes like the text itself – a motif – reminding the viewer that it is all an illusion constantly fitted into a rectangle ... into a picture frame, a film frame.

Since the film is deliberately built and shaped around the writing of the text of *The Tempest*, the script follows the play, act by act and scene by scene, with few transpositions and none of any substance to alter the chronology of the original. There have been some shortenings, the greatest being in the comedy scenes with Stephano and Trinculo. All other deletions have been made to service this particular cinematic presentation where action, location, continuity and detail have been considered more self-evident than they could be on a stage, and also to accommodate the particular characteristics of a production where Gielgud, for the most part, voices all the parts.

The film-script is very detailed. Its ambition is to attempt to inform everyone who has to use it – from those raising money to finance the film, to actors and extras, camera crew, costume designers, picture-researchers, painters, carpenters, set-dressers, soundmen, grips, lighting electricians, editing staff, advance buyers, distribution-organisers and publicists. It includes suggestive references to source material and unfilmable qualities like the smell of orange trees in the rain. Since the reading of scripts can be tedious, there is some evidence that it is written to be entertaining.

Prospero, homesick exile, has tried to recreate on his island many characteristics of a far distant Italy. In the building of his palaces, the stocking of his libraries, and in the fashioning of the indigenous spirits into classical allegories he has quoted extant buildings, paintings and books. Most of these are historical or contemporary to his life, but being a magician he can also slip time and borrow and quote the future. This script contains some examples of that referential source material in images which occasionally have been used in the manufacture of the film, though rarely will a direct visual quotation of a painting image be seen in the film.

The history of painting is one of borrowing and reprising, hommage and quotation. All image-makers who have wished to contribute to it have eagerly examined what painters have done before and – openly acknowledged or not – this huge body of pictorial work has become the legitimate and unavoidable encyclopedia for all to study and use. With hindsight and foresight, Prospero would have used it. So does *Prospero's Books*.

At its broadest organisation, the film is divided into Past, Present and Future: the Past corresponds to Prospero's long explanation of his history, the Present deals with Prospero's various real-time plottings and the Future concerns those plans Prospero makes to guarantee the success of his dynastic ambitions for his daughter. But it is most strongly structured into 91 sections, where each new section indicates a change in film-location. Each section is further broken down into numbered shots. Since films are rarely, if ever, filmed in chronological order, this section and shot breakdown enables the script to be conveniently reconstituted according to all the particular requirements of location filming. The shot numbers make for easy identification of detail, action and dialogue, with a multi-national cast and crew working variously in Amsterdam, Paris, Tokyo and London. The act and scene numbers of the original text are included to give a bearing to those who are familiar with the play from textbook reading and stage presentation.

Given the sophistication of the public towards film and television vocabulary, terms like wide-shot, medium-shot, close-up, back-light, top-light and slow-motion will be self-evident. In this film, a tracking shot – a sequence filmed from a moving camera – usually refers specifically to a camera on wheels being pushed or pulled on a dolly (a pneumatically-wheeled cart) by operators (called grips) across smooth and level open floor or, much more likely, along a length of temporary railway track that closely predetermines the camera's path and thus, for me, can minimise the camera becoming a subjective eye. Recourse to the use of tracks can limit a full 360-degree field of vision since the camera will probably, at some point, see the rails it is travelling on. Time, patience and ingenuity however can make sure that the tracks are disguised, hidden by props or, for the very energetic and those delighted by sleight of hand, swiftly assembled or dis-assembled as the camera approaches or retreats.

This film-script of *Prospero's Books* is published in much the same form as it was given to the film's producer, Kees Kasander, without whose support the existence of this *Tempest* adaption is not even a puff of wind far out at sea.

Film-making is a collaborative exercise on a grand scale and I would wish to thank all those hundreds of collaborators in Holland, Britain, France and Japan who have made *Prospero's Books* the film it is. I am sure that all of them would be happy to allow me to pick out two venerable gentlemen for especial thanks: Sacha Vierny and Sir John Gielgud, two master magicians of illusion.

Peter Greenaway, 1991

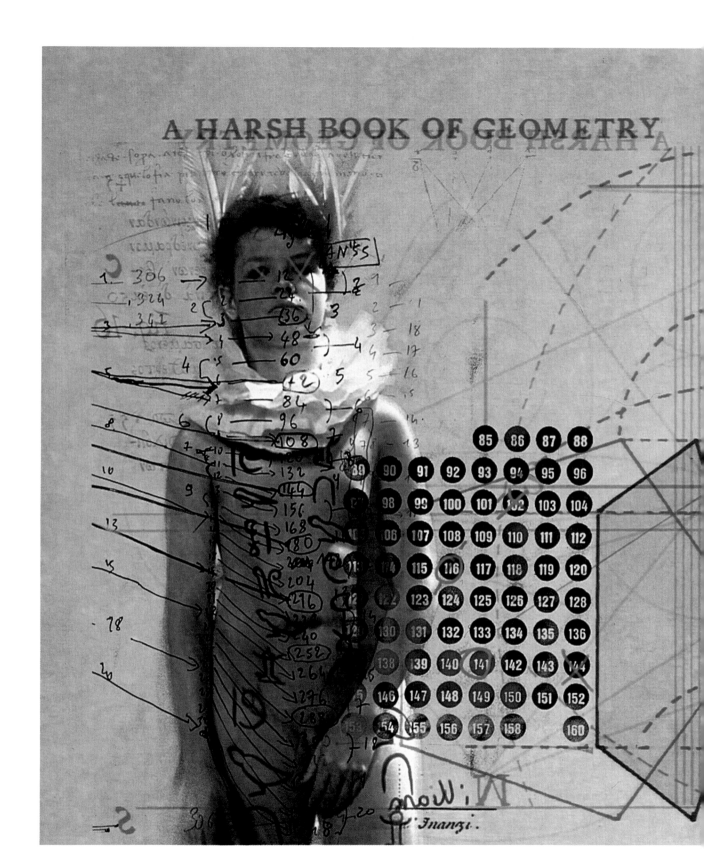

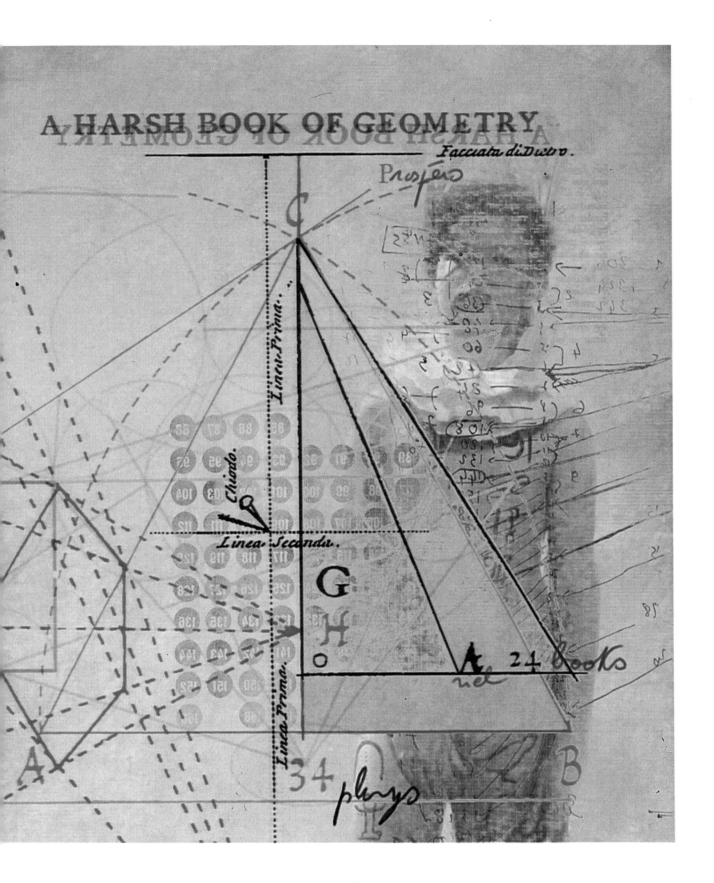

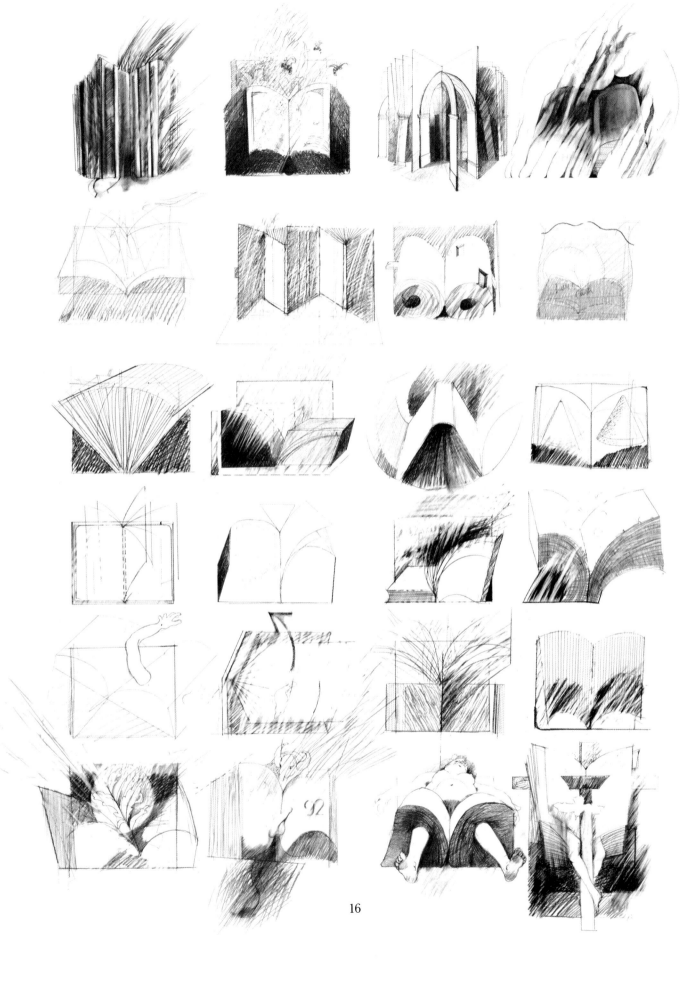

THE BOOKS

These are the twenty-four books that Gonzalo hastily threw into Prospero's boat as he was pushed out into the sea to begin his exile. These books enabled Prospero to find his way across the oceans, to combat the malignancies of Sycorax, to colonise the island, to free Ariel, to educate and entertain Miranda and to summon tempests and bring his enemies to heel.

1 *The Book of Water.* This is a waterproof-covered book which has lost its colour by much contact with water. It is full of investigative drawings and exploratory text written on many different thicknesses of paper. There are drawings of every conceivable watery association – seas, tempests, rain, snow, clouds, lakes, waterfalls, streams, canals, water-mills, shipwrecks, floods and tears. As the pages are turned, the watery elements are often animated. There are rippling waves and slanting storms. Rivers and cataracts flow and bubble. Plans of hydraulic machinery and maps of weather-forecasting flicker with arrows, symbols and agitated diagrams. The drawings are all made by one hand. Perhaps this is a lost collection of drawings by da Vinci bound into a book by the King of France at Amboise and bought by the Milanese Dukes to give to Prospero as a wedding present.

2 *A Book of Mirrors.* Bound in a gold cloth and very heavy, this book has some eighty shining mirrored pages; some opaque, some translucent, some manufactured with silvered papers, some coated in paint, some covered in a film of mercury that will roll off the page unless treated cautiously. Some mirrors simply reflect the reader, some reflect the reader as he was three minutes previously, some reflect the reader as he will be in a year's time, as he would be if he were a child, a woman, a monster, an idea, a text or an angel. One mirror constantly lies, one mirror sees the world backwards, another upside down. One mirror holds on to its reflections as frozen moments infinitely recalled. One mirror simply reflects another mirror across a page. There are ten mirrors whose purpose Prospero has yet to define.

3 *A Book of Mythologies.* This is a large book – Prospero on some occasions has described it as being as much as four metres wide and three metres high. It is bound in a shining yellow cloth that, when polished, gleams like brass. It is a compendium, in text and illustration, of mythologies with all their variants and alternative tellings; cycle after cycle of interconnecting tales of gods and men from all the known world, from the icy North to the deserts of Africa, with explanatory readings and symbolic interpretations. Its authority and information is richest in the Eastern Mediterranean, in Greece and Rome, in Israel, in Athens and Rome, Bethlehem and Jerusalem, where it supplements its information with genealogies, natural and unnatural. To a modern eye, it is a combination of Ovid's *Metamorphoses*, Frazer's *The Golden Bough* and Foxe's *Book of Martyrs*. Every tale and anecdote has an illustration. With this book as a concordance, Prospero can collect together, if he so wishes, all those gods and men who have achieved fame or infamy through water, or through fire, through deceit, in association with horses or trees or pigs or swans or mirrors, pride, envy or stick-insects.

4 *A Primer of the Small Stars.* This is a small, black, leather-covered navigational aid. It is full of folded maps of the night skies that tumble out, belying the modest size of the book. It is a depiction of the sky reflected in the seas of the world when they are still, for it is complete with blanks where the land masses of the globe have interrupted the oceanic mirror. This, to Prospero, was its greatest usage, for in steering his leaky vessel to such a small blank space in a sea of stars, he found his island. When opened, the primer's pages twinkle with travelling planets, flashing meteors and spinning

50

comets. The black skies pulsate with red numbers. New constellations are repeatedly joined together by fast-moving, dotted lines.

5 *An Atlas Belonging to Orpheus*. Bound in a battered and burnt, enamelled-green tin cover, this atlas is divided into two sections. Section One is full of large maps of the travel and usage of music in the classical world. Section Two is full of maps of Hell. It was used when Orpheus journeyed into the Underworld to find Eurydice, and the maps, as a consequence, are scorched and charred by Hellfire and marked with the teeth-bites of Cerberus. When the atlas is opened, the maps bubble with pitch. Avalanches of hot, loose gravel and molten sand fall out of the book to scorch the library floor.

6 *A Harsh Book of Geometry*. This is a thick, brown, leather-covered book, stippled with gold numbers. When opened, complex three-dimensional geometrical diagrams rise up out of the pages like models in a pop-up book. The pages flicker with logarithmic numbers and figures. Angles are measured by needle-thin metal pendulums that swing freely, activated by magnets concealed in the thick paper.

7 *The Book of Colours*. This is a large book bound in crimson watered silk. It is broader than it is high, and when opened the double-page spread makes a square. The three hundred pages cover the colour spectrum in finely differentiated shades moving from black back to black again. When opened at a double spread, the colour so strongly evokes a place, an object, a location or a situation that the associated sensory sensation is directly experienced. Thus a bright yellow-orange is an entry into a volcano and a dark blue-green is a reminder of deep sea where eels and fish swim and splash your face.

8 *The Vesalius Anatomy of Birth*. Vesalius produced the first authoritative anatomy book; it is astonishing in its detail, macabre in its single-mindedness. This *Anatomy of Birth*, a second volume now lost, is even more disturbing and heretical. It concentrates on the mysteries of birth. It is full of descriptive drawings of the workings of the human body which, when the pages open, move and throb and bleed. It is a banned book that queries the unnecessary processes of ageing, bemoans the wastages associated with progeneration, condemns the pains and anxieties of childbirth and generally questions the efficiency of God.

9 *An Alphabetical Inventory of the Dead*. This is a funereal volume, long and slim and bound in silver bark. It contains all the names of the dead who have lived on earth. The first name is Adam and the last is Susannah, Prospero's wife. The names are written in many inks and many calligraphies and are arranged in long columns that sometimes reflect the alphabet, sometimes a chronology of history, but often use taxonomies that are complicated to unravel, such that you may search many years to find a name, but be sure it will be there. The pages of the book are very old and are watermarked with a collection of designs for tombs and columbariums, elaborate headstones, graves, sarcophagi and other architectural follies for the dead, suggesting the book had other purposes, even before the death of Adam.

10 *A Book of Travellers' Tales*. This is a book that is much damaged, as though used a great deal by children who have treasured it. The scratched and rubbed crimson leather covers, once inlaid with a figurative gold design, are now so worn that the pattern is ambiguous and a fit subject for much speculation. It contains those marvels that travellers talk of and are not believed. 'Men whose heads stood in their breasts', 'bearded women, a rain of frogs, cities of purple ice, singing camels, Siamese twins', 'mountaineers dew-lapped like bulls'. It is full of illustrations and has little text.

11 *The Book of the Earth*. A thick book covered in khaki-coloured webbing, its pages are impregnated with the minerals, acids, alkalis, elements, gums, poisons, balms and aphrodisiacs of the earth. Strike a thick scarlet page with your thumbnail to summon fire. Lick a grey paste from another page to bring poisonous death. Soak a further page in water to cure anthrax. Dip another in milk to make soap. Rub two illustrated pages together to make acid. Lay your head on another page to change the colour of your hair. With this book Prospero savoured the geology of the island. With its help, he mined for salt and coal, water and mercury; and also for gold, not for his purse, but for his arthritis.

12 *A Book of Architecture and Other Music.* When the pages are opened in this book, plans and diagrams spring up fully-formed. There are definitive models of buildings constantly shaded by moving cloud-shadow. Noontime piazzas fill and empty with noisy crowds, lights flicker in noctural urban landscapes and music is played in the halls and towers. With this book, Prospero rebuilt the island into a palace of libraries that recapitulate all the architectural ideas of the Renaissance.

13 *The Ninety-Two Conceits of the Minotaur.* This book reflects on the experience of the Minotaur, the most celebrated progeny of bestiality. It has an impeccable classical mythology to explain provenances and pedigrees that include Leda, Europa, Daedalus, Theseus and Ariadne. Since Caliban – like centaurs, mermaids, harpies, the sphinx, vampires and werewolves – is the offspring of bestiality, he would find this book of great interest. Mocking Ovid's *Metamorphoses*, it tells the story of ninety-two hybrids. It should have told a hundred, but the puritanical Theseus had heard enough and slew the Minotaur before he could finish. When opened, the book exudes yellow steam and it coats the fingers with a black oil.

14 *The Book of Languages.* This is a large, thick book with a blue-green cover that rainbow-hazes in the light. More a box than a book, it opens in unorthodox fashion, with a door in its front cover. Inside is a collection of eight smaller books arranged like bottles in a medicine case. Behind these eight books are another eight books, and so on. To open the smaller books is to let loose many languages. Words and sentences, paragraphs and chapters gather like tadpoles in a pond in April or starlings in a November evening sky.

15 *End-plants.* Looking like a log of ancient, seasoned wood, this is a herbal to end all herbals, concerning itself with the most venerable plants that govern life and death. It is a thick block of a book with varnished wooden covers that have been at one time, and probably still are, inhabited by minute tunnelling insects. The pages are stuffed with pressed plants and flowers, corals and seaweeds, and around the book hover exotic butterflies, dragonflies, fluttering moths, bright beetles and a cloud of golden pollen-dust. It is simultaneously a honeycomb, a hive, a garden and an ark for insects. It is an encyclopedia of pollen, scent and pheromone.

16 *A Book of Love.* This is a small, slim, scented volume bound in red and gold, with knotted crimson ribbons for page-markers. There is certainly an image in the book of a naked man and a naked woman, and also an image of a pair of clasped hands. These things were once spotted, briefly, in a mirror, and that mirror was in another book. Everything else is conjecture.

17 *A Bestiary of Past, Present and Future Animals.* This is a large book, a thesaurus of animals, real, imaginary and apocryphal. With this book Prospero can recognise cougars and marmosets and fruitbats and manticores and dromersels, the cameleopard, the chimera and the cattamorrain.

18 *The Book of Utopias.* This is a book of ideal societies. With the front cover bound in gold leather and the back bound in black slate, it has five hundred pages, six hundred and sixty-six indexed entries and a preface by Sir Thomas

22

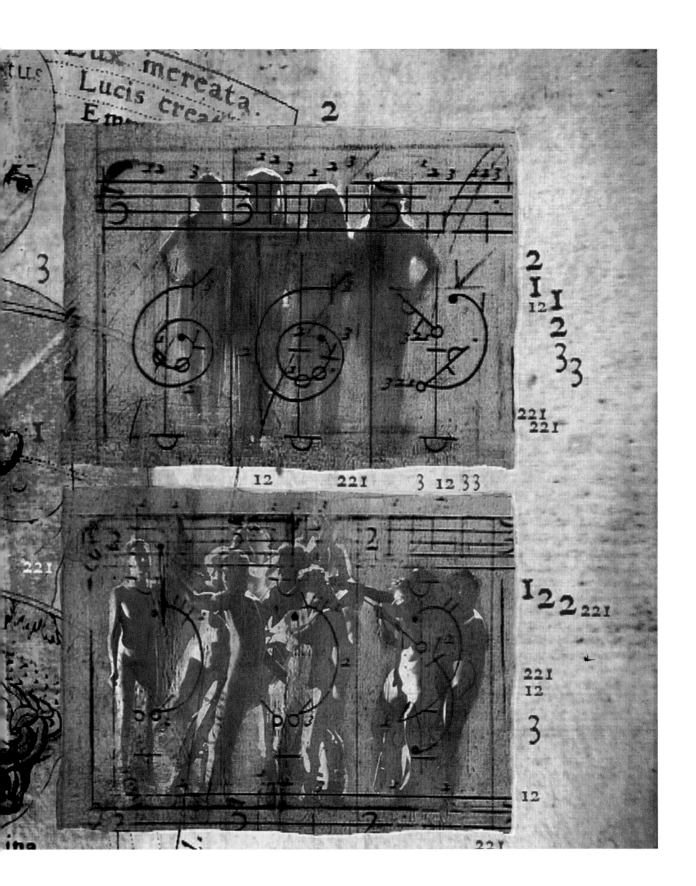

More. The first entry is a consensus description of Heaven and the last is one of Hell. There will always be someone on earth whose utopian ideal will be Hell. In the remaining pages of the book, every known and every imagined political and social community is described and evaluated, and twenty-five pages are devoted to tables where the characteristics of all societies can be isolated, permitting a reader to sort and match his own utopian ideal.

19 *The Book of Universal Cosmography.* Full of printed diagrams of great complexity, this book attempts to place all universal phenomena in one system. The diagrams are etched into the pages – disciplined geometrical figures, concentric rings that circle and countercircle, tables and lists organised in spirals, catalogues arranged on a simplified body of man, who, moving, sets the lists in new orders, moving diagrams of the solar system. The book deals in a mixture of the metaphorical and the scientific and is dominated by a great diagram showing the Union of Man and Woman – Adam and Eve – in a structured universe where all things have their allotted place and an obligation to be fruitful.

20 *Love of Ruins.* An antiquarian's handbook, a checklist of the ancient world for the Renaissance humanist interested in antiquity. Full of maps and plans of the archaeological sites of the world, temples, towns and ports, graveyards and ancient roads, measurements of one hundred thousand statues of Hermes, Venus and Hercules, descriptions of every discovered obelisk and pedestal of the Mediterranean, street plans of Thebes, Ostia and Atlantis, a directory of the possessions of Sejanus, the tablets of Heraclitus, the signatures of Pythagoras; an essential volume for the melancholic historian who knows that nothing endures. The book's proportions are like a block of stone, forty by thirty by twenty centimetres, the colour of blue-veined marble, chalky to the touch, with crisp, stiff pages printed in classical fonts with no W or J.

21 *The Autobiographies of Pasiphae and Semiramis* is a pornography. It is a blackened and thumbed volume whose illustrations leave small ambiguity as to the book's content. The book is bound in black calfskin with damaged lead covers. The pages are grey-green and scattered with a sludge-green powder, curled black hairs and stains of blood and other substances. The slightest taint of steam or smoke rises from the pages when the book is opened, and it is always warm – like the little heat apparent in drying plaster or in flat stones after the sun has set. The pages leave acidic stains on the fingers and it is advisable to wear gloves when reading the volume.

22 *A Book of Motion.* This is a book that at the most simple level describes how birds fly and waves roll, how clouds form and apples fall from trees. It describes how the eye changes its shape when looking at great distances, how hairs grow in a beard, why the heart flutters and the lungs inflate involuntarily and how laughter changes the face. At its most complex level, it explains how ideas chase one another in the memory and where thought goes when it is finished with. It is covered in tough blue leather and, because it is always bursting open of its own volition, it is bound around with two leather straps buckled tightly at the spine. At night, it drums against the bookcase shelf and has to be held down with a brass weight. One of its sections is called 'The Dance of Nature' and here, codified and explained in animated drawings, are all the possibilities for dance in the human body.

23 *The Book of Games.* This is a book of board games of infinite supply. Chess is but one game in a thousand in this volume, merely occupying two pages, pages 112 and 113. The book contains board games to be played with counters and dice, with cards and flags and miniature pyramids, small figures of the Olympic gods, the winds in coloured glass, Old Testament prophets in bone, Roman busts, the oceans of the world, exotic animals, pieces of coral, gold putti, silver coins and pieces of liver. The board games represented in the book cover as many situations as there are experiences. There are games of death, resurrection, love, peace, famine, sexual cruelty, astronomy, the cabbala, statesmancraft, the stars, destruction, the future, phenomenology, magic, retribution, semantics, evolution. There are boards of red and black triangles, grey and blue diamonds, pages of text, diagrams of the brain, Arabic carpets, boards in the shape of the constellations, animals, maps, journeys to Hell and journeys to Heaven.

24 *Thirty-Six Plays.* This is a thick, printed volume of plays dated 1623. All thirty-six plays are there save one – the first. Nineteen pages are left blank for its inclusion. It is called *The Tempest.* The folio collection is modestly bound in dull green linen with cardboard covers and the author's initials are embossed in gold on the cover – W.S.

THE BOOK OF

carnation

Ceres' bless... ...you

397

COLOURS

398.

aqua cerulean

why hath thy queen
Summon'd me hither

THE PAINTBOX IMAGES

The script of *Prospero's Books* calls for the manufacture of magical volumes that embody their contents beyond text and conventional illustration. Prospero, sixteenth-century scholar and magus, would no doubt call upon the most contemporary state-of-the-art techniques that the legacy of the Gutenberg revolution could offer. The newest Gutenberg technology – and to talk of a comparable revolution may not be to exaggerate – is the digital, electronic Graphic Paintbox. This machine, as its name suggests, links the vocabulary of electronic picture-making with the traditions of the artist's pen, palette and brush, and like them permits a personal signature. I believe its possibilities could radically affect cinema, television, photography, painting and printing (and maybe much else), allowing them to reach degrees of sophistication not before considered. Although the paintbox can be seen as a collaging tool of which Schwitters and Heartfield would have been envious, the image-manipulation it makes possible cannot satisfactorily be contained in the word collage. For the paintbox can change the shape, form, contrast, colour, tone, texture, ratio and scale of any given material, then store the resulting infinite solutions for reappraisal. With additional equipment, this material can then be reproduced as film, as audio-tape and as still-photograph. If uniqueness is considered desirable, it is possible to make a unique image. If infinite reproduction is required, then as far as the digital paintbox is concerned, there is no fear of quality loss. No special technical ability is necessary to operate the machine and competent familiarity can be achieved quickly. However, its potential, as always, depends on the audacity, imagination and pictorial sophistication of the user.

The paintbox operator sits at a table in front of a large television monitor and holds an electronic stylus of familiar pen-like shape and usage above an acutely sensitive electronic pad. On the screen is a menu of functions: select, draw, paint, brush-size, chalk, stencil, cut-out, lay-out, delete, browse, restore, save, overlay, flood, airbrush, mask, erase; there is access to archive and library, and to a palette from which colours can be mixed to an infinite number of nuances.

The film of *Prospero's Books* acknowledges its many sources in a text written by a late-sixteenth-century English dramatist whose business was illusion and theatre, who wrote about an Italian scholar beholden to books, a man whose imaginative world came from his researches into Greek, Roman and Renaissance scholarship. In the making of the film, there has been an attempt to find those processes at work in image as well as in text. Many of these images concern the indigenous spirits of the island that Prospero has refashioned to suit his Renaissance scholarship. One of them is The Juggler, a one-sixth-part attempt to fathom the nature of the Fool, but like all the creatures on the island she had other roles before the advent of Prospero's colonial rule.

THE JUGGLER

'Prospero wanted a Fool to enliven his morning procession. He wanted to have some wit about him; someone fearlessly to cauterise his soul with home truths. He could not find one. It was too difficult a post and too irksome a responsibility. The available material, though willing, was not sophisticated enough to hold the opposing characteristics and the contradictory talents. So Prospero split the Foolish Allegory into six parts.

'Why do you laugh at a fool? You laugh at a clever and showy skill. A jester is adroit and plays skilful games. He might juggle. A juggler needs a facility of balance, a quickness of hand and a desire to deceive the eye.'

'Prospero looked for jugglers. He looked for twinkling eyes and the smell of sweat and pepper, for he remembered a Milanese court entertainer who had just those characteristics. After a quick appraisal, for Prospero could not be seen to spend too long on such a humble appointment, the most likely candidate proved to be a naked, bright-orange bacchante with wide hips who juggled balls and fruit, scientific instruments and defenceless small animals. But Prospero did not know that he had picked an immigrant. She had been a stowaway in the boat left by the sailors who had brought the disgraced, blue-eyed, big-bellied belly-dancer Sycorax. Just like Prospero, Sycorax had been sent into exile. But Sycorax had carnally consorted with the Devil. Had Prospero carnally consorted with the Devil? Only the Devil in books. This juggler had juggled figures for the Algerian witch. She had been her book-keeper, her cabbalistic counter, her numbers advocate.

'For Prospero, this little laughing, orange, juggling creature played the juggling part during the day but was a professional fornicator at night. Maybe the roles were interchangeable. She dyed her body orange by laying in a wet iron-pit and her partners soon knew each other. Every marked fornicator could see so many others on the beach each morning. The juggler's eagerness to please Prospero in her diurnal role eventually affected her nocturnal fee. For she asked her satyrical clients for objects to juggle with, preferably brightly-coloured, for she had a notion that Prospero had been colour-blinded by reading too many black-and-white books. She savoured the eccentric object, a potato shaped like a dwarf's foot, a pebble with holes like eyes, a Venus fruit-nut scarred to suggest rape, a petrified apple bitten by Eve.

'And then a reversal occurred. She began to exchange her roles. Trying to annexe quality in her nocturnal clientele by exhibitions of her skill, she juggled with mathematical solids, splashing herself with her own stale milk, fearful that her orange body could not be seen among the dark columned corridors. The clients grew bored and moved to other pastures to browse their sensual taste. To distract her from her ellipses of circulating dizziness, she was left only with the very old, the very young and the very simple-minded.

'Continuing to confuse her responsibilities, she began to accept professional advances by day, especially from the lazy, imitation scholars who ought to have been pretending to read the books in the alchemical section of Prospero's library. Finally she perfected juggling and fornicating by day and by night as simultaneous activities. In disappointed exasperation, Prospero turned his head the other way and sought his Fool elsewhere.'

To provide a background for many possible images in the film, a library of some thousand or more small 'field frames' was made – each some 8 by 6 centimetres – painted or drawn on paper in various media – paint, ink, graphite, pastel – in sequential book-form, stressing the painterly characteristics of mass, volume and colour in preference to line. Because these images were comparatively small, the enlargement necessary to make them useful also enlarged the grain and texture of the paper thereby stressing their manufacture. The picture ratio of the new Hi-Vision television image is approximately 1 to 1.78 – a landscape ratio beginning to approach the dimensions of the cinemascope-screen (conventional television monitors have a ratio of 1 to 1.33), so the first step in the manufacture of the portrait-image of The Juggler – was to record the selected field frame on a Hi-Definition rostrum camera and refashion and rebuild it to fit the 1.78 ratio of the new screen. This process is swiftly managed on the paintbox by selecting desirable areas of colour and texture out of the frame and re-positioning and blending them. Sections of the textured framing of the original small drawing can literally be 'picked up', duplicated and re-deposited to extend the new framing, without in any way diminishing or deteriorating the sections by their removal.

Satisfied, for the moment, with the new shaped field-frame (though infinite subsequent alterations are possible), a coloured 35mm photographic transparency taken of a film-extra personifying The Juggler, is re-photographed on to tape

29

on the rostrum camera linked with the paintbox. The image is electronically cropped to be used twice. First it is enlarged three times to be used in the left foreground of the image and then, decreased by fifty per cent, it is placed in the right midground. These two newly fashioned images are then arranged independently – and with as much touch precision as required. Any extraneous material that surrounds the waist-high portrait of the smiling orange woman can be cut, cropped, shaded away, re-coloured or re-blended to emphasise her presence. Obelisk-ornaments from the library behind the smaller woman's head have been left to provide links to the later architectural additions. Since the description of the allegorical creature concerns her dual rules as night-time fornicator and day-time juggler, the larger foreground image is blackened and masked by selecting black graphite texture from a field-frame, and scumbling it on her face in varying degrees of thickness using different sized 'electronic' brush-sizes. As much time and detailing as is considered necessary can be used to apply the texturing and, if the result is not satisfactory, then the effects can be effortlessly wiped and the process restarted without interference to the already existing material – a unique facility not encountered in other image-making experiences. When the night and day-time figures of The Juggler are completed – their relevance to one another and to the total image can be adjusted in tone and contrast, by masking techniques and colour adjustments.

Architectural space and architectural cultural reference on Prospero's rebuilt island are suggested by the collaging of a Piranesi print of grandiose architecture into the image. The black-and-white print quality of the original is retained to emphasise the notion of it being a quoted reference – Prospero is acknowledged in the film as an eclectic architectural scholar, perfectly capable of prophetic borrowing (Piranesi wasn't born till 1720, some 161 years after Prospero's island landing in 1559). To place the architecture in the same space as the two figures, the nearer columns have been brushed in with the orange colour 'lifted' from the base of the image itself. With the electronic stylus now used directly as a sharply-nibbed pen, to acknowledge The Juggler's determination to be seen in the dark, the ivy-wreath leaves in her hair are outlined in a manufactured dark blue, and then, on command, filled or 'flooded' with a flat, matt white. The whole is again toned in with more black 'graphite' scumbling to prevent the sharp white addition jumping forward or creating optical 'holes' in the picture-surface.

A distant – and very slightly blasphemous – reference to the architectural framework of a traditional sacra conversazione as painted by Bellini or Mantegna (two serious painters of allegory) sections of the grey frame are taken from the partially manufactured image and reconstructed around the second Juggler's head. She is thus provided with a frame for a line of text spoken by Caliban expressing the true feelings felt by the island spirits towards Prospero's colonial rule. Emphasis is given to the main sentiment of the sentence by casting it in an easily legible dark blue, the colour of Prospero's identifying cloak. The secondary message of the sentence is coloured in bright red, Caliban's colour of violence and carnality which is less readable, being partially camouflaged against the background, reflecting Caliban's fear of exposure as a malcontent. Other textural resonances are 'juggled' with in the word 'rootedly'. The printed text itself – with its distressed font – is a direct quotation photographed and enlarged from a fascimile edition of the 1623 folio of Shakespeare's plays – the first known source of the complete Shakespeare opus of 36 works that has *The Tempest* as its first play. As regards the film, to use the Shakespearean posthumous printed text in this way is an especial irony, since Prospero is seen writing the text of *The Tempest* with a truncated quill, precursor of the electric stylus, producing a longhand manuscript that – like all other Shakespearean manuscripts – has never been seen. The film's ending interferes with chronology and history and plays a game with this loss that is lamented by every Shakespearean enthusiast.

To imply a continuity with the other five parts of the Fool . . . simpleton, pedant, prig, pimp and drunk . . . a residue of the fascimile folio text is seen creeping off into the next frame where the significance of the letters will be demonstrated.

To complete the smiling bogus portrait of The Juggler further, she holds two hand-sized balls, conventionalised attributes of her juggling and her sexual services, but converted into flat-colour, 'unjuggleable' discs – representing the day and the night sky – the two opposites of her working role as nocturnal fornicator and daytime juggler . . . and by a further 'unjuggleable' open framework red cube. It is here placed in its own private space beneath a dimly seen orrery from the original library photograph – a three-dimensional model of the juggling of the planets caught in a frozen moment . . . operated by Prospero's Providence, the Great Juggler . . . and indication . . . if by now indication is needed – of The Juggler's original role as Sycorax's numerologist and geometrician. All of which is a nicely tuned conceit to illuminate the role of deception implied by Prospero's magic and by the illusion and deception practised by a playwright . . . and maybe by a film-maker in the manufacture of cinema, and maybe indeed practised by a film-maker in his description of the manufacture of an image.

The paintbox image of The Juggler appears on pages 30/31.
The other paintbox images shown here are:
A Book of Water (10/11), The Harsh Book of Geometry (14/15),
The Autobiography of Pasiphae and Semiramis (18/19),
The Book of Motion (22/23), The Book of Colours (26/27)
and The Ninety-Two Conceits of the Minotaur (34/35).

34

THE PAST

THE FILM-SCRIPT OF *PROSPERO'S BOOKS* HAS BEEN DIVIDED INTO THREE LARGE BUT UNEQUAL SECTIONS, PAST, PRESENT AND FUTURE. THIS FIRST PART DEALS LARGELY WITH PROSPERO RELATING HIS HISTORY BOTH TO US, THE AUDIENCE, AND TO MIRANDA, HIS FIFTEEN-YEAR-OLD DAUGHTER. IT REPRESENTS, IN A SENSE, THE 'STORY SO FAR'. AS MANY NARRATIVE EVENTS HAPPEN IN THIS FIRST PART AS IN ALL THE OTHER PARTS OF THE SCRIPT PUT TOGETHER. THE STORY-TELLING IS QUICK-MOVING AND EPISODIC, WITH ELABORATE AND ILLUSIVE FRAMINGS, DELIBERATE CONFUSIONS BETWEEN FACT, MEMORY AND FANTASY, AND WITH LIGHTING THAT IS BASICALLY DARK AND RICHLY COLOURED, INFLUENCED BY LATE-SEVENTEENTH-CENTURY ITALIAN AND DUTCH PAINTING OF INTERIORS.

DA VINCI WAS AN INDEFATIGABLE ENTHUSIAST FOR THE QUALITY, MOTION AND SUBSTANCE OF
WATER AND AN IDEAL AUTHORITY TO CONSULT IN THE CREATION OF A TEMPEST.

ACT I SCENE I
SECTION 1
THE BATH-HOUSE

1.1 Much magnified and in slow-motion . . . a drop of back-lit water splashes into a black pool. The noise of its splash is loud and abrupt.

1.2 Pages in a book called *The Book of Water* are turned – there are drawings of seas, rain, clouds, sleet, snow. The book is large and each page contains handwritten texts and illustrations. The water connections are inventive. It is a speculative textbook of 1611 – interested in metaphysics as well as terrestrial physics. A collection of drawings on different paper in different inks bound together to make a book – perhaps it is a collection of lost da Vinci drawings.

1.3 A second drop of water splashes into a black pool - the splash sets up secondary splashes – the image recalls a dispassionate scientific study of water behaving inexorably as water.

1.4 More pages of the book are turned. There are drawings of whirlpools, hydraulics, diagrams of the Archimedes Screw, water rushing in gutters, waterfalls and cataracts, snow crystals, irrigation channels and canals.

One of the drawings is animated – small black arrows drawn in perspective rotate within the outlines of a whirlpool.

1.5 A third drop of water splashes into the black pool. Its splash echoes for many seconds.

1.6 More pages are turned . . . there are illustrations of climate – storms, high winds, hurricanes and tempests.

More drawings are animated. Slanting lines of animated rain sweep over choppy water.

1.7 A fourth drop of water falls . . . this time into a shallow pool of water held in the cupped hand of an old man.

1.8 More pages are turned to show . . . compassionate drawings of floods, the Flood, Noah and the Ark, details of people in swirling water, tragic heads bobbing in tempestuous seas, drowning, bodies washed around in the Deep and shipwrecks.

The text – though neatly written – is not easily legible. Maybe it is readable when viewed in a mirror. Some of the images are animated – a wave moves, a ripple-motion animates the drawing of an ebbing tide, animated colour sweeps through the black-and-white drawing of a waterfall, a real corpse is buffeted by moving water in an image of the Flood and real tears travel down a woman's face.

1.9 An elderly man . . . like a de la Tour St Jerome . . . like a Bellini St Anthony . . . stands white and naked in a bath-house. He is the centre of the picture . . . his hair is ruffled at the back of his head. Although vulnerable and decidedly mortal in his

age and nakedness, he makes a dignified image. Flecked and speckled by dazzling water-reflections that are so bright they hurt the eye . . . in the act of washing . . . he has paused with amusement and perhaps scientific speculation to catch the water-droplets that fall from the high, dark, domed vault above his head. Beside him, standing in the water, is an ornate table . . . on it is a collection of large, exotic shells and a basin and brushes, sponges and towels. This old man is Prospero.

1.10 In slow-motion, another drop of water splashes in Prospero's cupped hand.

1.11 The water drops – in slow-motion – fall out of the blackness of a domed, darkened ceiling. They fall in such slow-motion that they look like drops of dangerous ectoplasm falling towards the camera and just missing it (and us). The drops are back-lit and – steadily – they begin to drip with increasing speed.

1.12 The elderly man watches the drops hit and splash in his hand.

As an exiled scholar in the wilderness, this de la Tour St Jerome offers a very mortal image for Prospero stripped and humbled before a book.

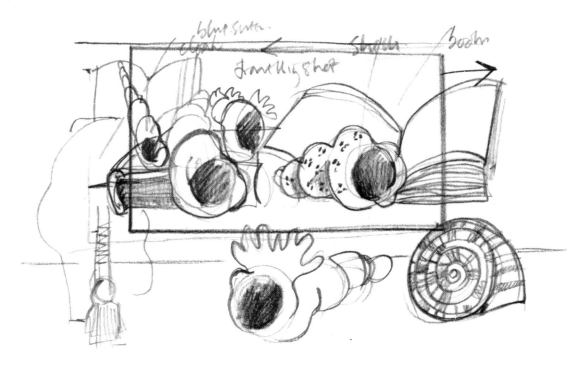

PROSPERO, MORTAL AND VULNERABLE IN THE DARK SPACES OF HIS BATH-HOUSE, DREAMS OF
THE REVERSAL OF HIS FORTUNES.

1.13 A travelling wide shot. The bath-house is classical/mannerist – a personal, idiosyncratic, exhibitionistic view of classicism. There are many, many columns – plain and unfluted – with undecorated or negligibly-decorated capitals – and through them and among them – many long, regular, mathematically-exact perspectives – like exercises in perspective-drawing. The sound of the steadily falling drops echoes along these stone perspectives.

PROSPERO'S 'POOR CELL' IS AN IRONY. WITH
HIS MAGIC PROSPERO CAN BUILD HIS
OWN ARCHITECTURAL CAPRICCIOS SCALED
PROPHETICALLY TO PIRANESI'S ROMANTICISM.

Prospero stands in the bath – in shallow water which reaches to his knees. The water is lit from beneath – with a green and white light whose reflections shimmer and glimmer on to the columns. On the stone, flagged floor beside the pool . . . a docile elderly lion is stretched out on its belly . . . there are piles of books on stone benches . . . and a collection of mathematical solids – a cube, a pyramid, a sphere, a hexagon, octahedron, decahedron . . . .

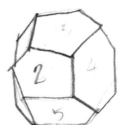

The camera sees all these things and then travels closer to the table standing in the bath . . . a wooden chair stands by the table. On the table . . . are several thick volumes. One of them, the book we have been looking at – *The Book of Water* – is propped open on a small lectern. The book is large – some 50 by 40 centimetres and 6 centimetres thick – it has a thick binding washed and drained of colour – perhaps it was originally blue . . . maybe green – a waterproofed cover – impervious to the world's water getting in and the book's water getting out.

There is also a pile of Prospero's clothes – including a large, black-brown cloak that sparkles a little with an elaborate pattern of dark beads and metal thread. The cloak has tassels and cords and looks heavy and cumbersome to wear.

1.14 The naked, white figure of Prospero slowly turns the pages of *The Book of Water* with his right hand . . . whilst the water-drops splash into his outstretched left hand. A child's voice sings.

1.15 We see the source of the singing. Sitting on the bath-side – near the lion – is a small and handsome, naked, male child – aged maybe six, seven, eight? He dabbles his feet in the water. The water reflections ripple back over his face and body. He is like the dancing child in Bronzino's 'Allegory of Venus, Cupid, Folly and Time'.

LOOKING FOR AN IMAGE OF ARIEL,
THIS ALLEGORY BY BRONZINO OF VENUS,
CUPID, FOLLY AND TIME OFFERS AN
IMAGE OF THE SPIRIT OF AIR AS A
CURLY-HEADED CHILD BENT ON
RECKLESS, DANGEROUS IMPUDENCE.

1.16 Prospero's left index finger stops its wandering on the page of the book at the paragraph of indecipherable handwriting and a small design of tempestuous waves . . . a design with arrows and dotted lines and numbers . . . and including a ship, an ink-drawn galleon made insignificant by the waves. The galleon cannot be much larger than a thumbnail. Prospero's finger comes to rest beside it . . . the arrows and the dotted lines and the numbers move . . . the numbers flick over, the arrows zig-zag.

The numbers and arrows and figures are attracted to Prospero's finger . . . they leave the page and glide and roll across his fingernail; they rotate and circle – gain colour and flash and sparkle. Where the pressure of the finger is strongest on the page, so there the activity is greatest. Prospero's finger creates a vortex and a whirlpool of diagrammatic action.

1.17 In medium-shot – Prospero is smiling . . . then gently and experimentally – in the quietest of whispers . . . he mouths some words ruminatively . . . curiously . . . interrogatively.

PROSPERO (playing the Master of the Ship):
Boatswain!

At once, far off . . . begins a rumbling, droning noise – like a thousand distant flying machines – like the sound of an armada of mechanical birds – a noise reminiscent of implacable, massive stage machinery in a masque or pageant that is several streets away. It is not one sound but many sounds combined. This is the sound of Prospero's magic. It always precedes every act of magic that Prospero performs and is the slow prelude – ever increasing in noise – that always prefaces a massive burst of aggressively 'musical' sound when the peak of the magic is attained.

SECTION 2
PROSPERO'S STUDY

2.1 For four seconds, a large close-up of the word 'Boatswain', handwritten on a blank sheet of crisp off-white paper, fills the screen . . . the camera is close enough to see the texture of the paper and to watch the black and shining ink slowly dry. For the moment, there is no clue whatsoever where this handwritten word on paper is situated.

SECTION 3
THE BATH-HOUSE

3.1 Close-up. In the bath-house, Prospero experimentally savours the word 'Boatswain' a second time – this time a little louder.

3.2   In wide-shot. Prospero says the word 'Boatswain' a third time and is watched by the benign and smiling child – who is Ariel. The sound of the approach of Prospero's magic is getting louder.

SECTION 4
PROSPERO'S STUDY

4.1   For six seconds, there is a large close-up of the word 'Boatswain' being written . . . this time we glimpse the nib of the pen that is writing on crisp off-white paper . . . the ink dries and a shadow falls across the paper. We do not know where this writing activity is taking place.

SECTION 5
THE BATH-HOUSE

5.1   In the bath-house, Ariel, the benign and smiling child, stands and watches Prospero – who, prompted by the water dripping from the ceiling and by the illustrated *Book of Water* – begins to conjure the idea of a scenario for a storm by using a single word. He now says the word 'Boatswain' quite audibly.

5.2   Prospero begins to develop the drama. A close-up of the wry face of the smiling Prospero.

PROSPERO (playing the Boatswain):
Here, Master. What cheer?

The sound of Prospero's magic increases. Its ultimate power and magnitude is now to be guessed at – it is an intimidating sound.

SECTION 6
PROSPERO'S STUDY

6.1   Beneath the word 'Boatswain' – written on the white page – we see the words that Prospero has just spoken – 'Here, Master. What cheer?'
The shot is wider than before, and the off-white page is seen to be the page of a thick book full of white, unwritten pages. And the hand that holds the pen is also seen – the hand of an old man. It is Prospero's hand. We catch a glimpse of a dark-blue, brocaded sleeve – wherever Prospero is, he is not writing in the bath-house.

SECTION 7
THE BATH-HOUSE

7.1   In the bath-house, Prospero, standing in the water, expands on his ruminations.

PROSPERO:
Boatswain, speak to the mariners.

After – experimentally – mouthing these words, Prospero lifts his head to listen . . . as though perhaps waiting for a distant reply.

7.2   A wide shot. Along the distant perspectives of columns comes a draught that lifts thin drapes and ruffles the water of the bath. There is a flickering of distant light – lightning . . . and above the rumbling of the noise of Prospero's magic – an audible distant grumble of thunder. Prospero and Ariel look along the perspective of columns from where the sound is coming. The shadows on the columns of the bath-house darken.

SECTION 8
PROSPERO'S STUDY

8.1.   More is now revealed of the book in which Prospero is writing his new text. A medium shot shows a head-to-waist view of Prospero sitting at a large wooden desk – surrounded by shelves of books and curios – fossils, small statuettes and writing materials. Prospero wears a large, heavy, dark-blue cloak or gown that enfolds him like a quilted blanket . . . it is darkly embroidered with small wine-coloured beads and swirls of black vegetation . . . it has long strings and ornate tassels that trail to the ground . . . it is a garment that has often been worn . . . a little frayed and scuffed. Later it will be seen to be capable of changing colour . . . in seven stages comparable to the power of Prospero's magic . . . black, brown, dark blue, light blue, purple, dark red and fiery red . . . and to have a vivid lining embroidered with dazzling stars – a lining that is only revealed in flashes as when a dark butterfly momentarily uncovers coloured underwings.

On the desk in front of Prospero . . . on top of a small pile of books is a small model ship . . .

8.2 Close-up. The model ship . . . a galleon made of precious metals . . . a three-masted, fully-rigged king's flagship . . . exactly like the one drawn in *The Book of Water* seen in the bath-house . . . the model is finely made . . . as though manufactured by a jeweller or a goldsmith . . . as though manufactured by Cellini.

8.3 Prospero's expression is wry and contemplative. He stares at the model ship, then dips his pen in a dish of ink that looks like black mercury, and he writes.

8.4 In close-up, we read what Prospero writes: 'Fall to it, yarely, or we run ourselves aground!'

SECTION 9
THE BATH-HOUSE

9.1 In the bath-house, Prospero says the words we have just seen written . . . in fact, before the words have finished being written, Prospero is saying them.

PROSPERO:
Fall to it, yarely, or we run ourselves aground!

He amuses himself with the nautical terminology.

9.2 There is a close-up of Prospero's cupped hand where the drops of water fall . . . and in his palm is the small, exquisitely-made, yellow, three-masted, fully-rigged, model galleon – in its small puddle of hand-held water.

9.3 An even closer close-up shows the water-drops – in slow-motion – falling on the diminutive ship – on its rigging, its sails, its decks . . .

PROSPERO (playing the Master of the Ship):
Fall to it, yarely, or we run ourselves aground!
Bestir, bestir!

9.4 Prospero looks at Ariel and makes an almost imperceptible gesture – a questioning turn of the head – for his support in the scenario. Ariel smiles.

9.5 Prospero looking closely at the model ship in his hand . . .

PROSPERO (playing the Boatswain):
Heigh, my hearts! Cheerly, cheerly, my hearts! Take in the topsail. Tend to the Master's whistle.

He looks up at Ariel.

9.6 The child smiles and stands and, holding his small penis like an ornamental water-spout – he sends an arc of crystal-clear, backlit water into the shallow bath. The sound of this arc of water hitting the water in the bath is crisply audible above the thunder-rumble and the sound of Prospero's magic which continues to build up in the echoic background.

9.7 Prospero blows into his cupped hand.

PROSPERO:
Blow, till thou burst thy wind, if room enough!

He says the words with mock vehemence.

SEATED AT HIS WRITING DESK BEFORE A MODEL GALLEON AND THE BOOK OF WATER,
PROSPERO CONCEIVES THE STORM.

SECTION 10
PROSPERO'S STUDY

10.1 We see the words – handwritten in black ink on the page: 'Blow, till thou burst thy wind, if room enough!'

With a swift circling motion – to match the strength and suggestion of space of the words – the camera retreats from the page and circles round to show Prospero at his desk in a wide shot. More of Prospero's study is revealed. It is apparent that he is seated in a constructed wooden study where the seat and the desk and the shelves are part of a whole designed unit – the whole provided with different curtained alcoves – some of the curtains are drawn, some half-drawn, some wide open. What is beyond the curtains is not yet apparent. Many more books and artefacts are revealed – and there are herbal plants in ceramic pots, a vase of peacock feathers, candlesticks, chained volumes. The whole is lit by a mellow, orange Rembrandtian light. The open white book that rests on the sloping desk and in which Prospero is writing . . . appears to throw up a white glare on to his face.

10.2 Mid-shot. Prospero takes a book from a large pocket in his cloak. He opens it. It is *A Book of Mirrors*. The mirror-pages flash reflections back into his face and around his study. Each page has a mirrored surface.

10.3 Close-up on the book. As the pages turn – some are dull, some opaque, some shining, some almost transparent so that they look like smeared window-glass, some are spotted with age, some scratched, some look like polished tin or bronze, others seem dark and impenetrable. Prospero finds a page and holds it steady – it reflects his head and shoulders and behind him – we can see something else – not a reflection of his study but a group of figures sodden with rain standing in a downpour of water. Momentarily – as we watch – Prospero's reflection disappears, revealing the rain-drenched figures standing alone – it is a pre-saging of the mirror-images of the film – starting at Shot 11.5.

SECTION 11
THE BATH-HOUSE

11.1   In the bath-house, the small yellow ship in Prospero's hand trembles before the approach of his breath. In scale, his breath is a mighty storm.

11.2   Looking up at the ceiling above his head – which is now flecked in dark shadows and dark wisps of billowing smoke – Prospero continues his dramatic and whispered scenario.

PROSPERO (playing Alonso):
Good boatswain, have care. Where's the Master?
Play the men.
(playing the Boatswain):
I pray now, keep below.
(playing Antonio):
Where is the Master, boatswain?
(playing the Boatswain):
Do you not hear him? You mar our labour. Keep your cabins. You do assist the storm.

11.3   Prospero – now more than ever dramatically lit from the sparkling lights of the pool – sets the diminutive boat on the water of the bath. It trembles and bucks in the rough water caused by the peeing Ariel . . .

11.4   Prospero sits down in his chair that stands in the glittering water. He looks at the little ship floating on the choppy water . . . and his eyes harden.

PROSPERO (playing the Boatswain):
What care these roarers for the name of the King?

The last word is almost explosively shouted – with a ring of anger and sarcasm and contempt. Prospero, for the first time, drops his mockery and his play-acting and permits himself (and us) a real show of his feelings.

11.5   As Prospero sits in his chair . . . he conjures up an image.

Mirror-image: This is to be the first of a great many such conjured images.

At a later stage the device to 'hold' the image will be more defined – here . . . for the first time . . . it seems to be an image in a mirror held slightly askew from the picture-plain. The mirror is apparently held by dark, almost unseen, black figures – dark-fleshed, ambiguously-sexed, naked – they splash in the water of the bath – and they strain and grunt to hold up their large heavy mirror . . . as though this first conjured image of Prospero's imagining is tortuously arrived at.

Later this device of mirror and mirror-carriers will be developed and many changes rung from its possibilities. When the image in the mirror is optimistic, the mirror-carriers will be light-skinned, handsome, young . . . and the mirror easy and light to lift. When the image is pessimistic, its carriers will be haggard, ugly, misshapen and dark, and the mirror heavy and burdensome. These figures will be more and more revealed until the idea is made

decorative frame

book.

pill box

and round.

cut away

concrete that Prospero's imaginings – good and bad, fair and foul – are always 'reflected' in mirrors held by minions – minions and spirits of a Roman/Greek/Renaissance mythology . . . as though a mirror was always necessary for Prospero to make his imaginings manifest.

On this occasion, the mirror-bearers (fading swiftly into their places – with a locked-on camera trick?) are standing in the bath-water beside and a little behind Prospero . . . and they lift their heavy mirror from a horizontal position under the water to a vertical position just above the water-surface . . . water-droplets run down the full length of the mirror and drip back into the bath.

We first see the seated Prospero reflected in the carried mirror . . . and then with a flash, the mirror changes through a slight angle and we see what Prospero sees in his mind's eye . . . in this case it is an image of the victims of the storm Prospero is conjuring up . . . an image of silhouetted figures in a yellow downpour of torrential rain – they are totally besodden – their hair stuck to their faces, their clothing glued to their backs – they huddle open-mouthed in the storm.

They are framed to the knee with rain-sodden darkness behind them. (Perhaps these victims of the storm – differently-lit – can stand – just out of frame – in the same bath-water as Prospero – with their yellow-black light reaching out and shining on Prospero . . .?)

(*Question*: Perhaps this sort of artifice can sometimes be seen for what it is – in this case the camera pulling back to see Prospero staring at his mirror-image and we – as audience – comprehending how it is done – as though Prospero can only realise his imagination in a mirror – making us, the audience privy to a greater, more magical world than he is. An opportunity to demonstrate the cinema's illusionism and artifice at the same time.)

PROSPERO (voice-over):
To cabin! Silence! Trouble us not.

The figures back away. Prospero gives them voices.

PROSPERO (playing Gonzalo):
Remember whom thou hast aboard.
(playing the Boatswain):
None that I love more than myself. If you can command these elements to silence, and work the peace of the present, we will not hand a rope more.

The mirror-bearers lay the mirror down into a horizontal position in the water again . . . on the way – by angling the mirror – catching Prospero's reflection – and then (with a device of a locked-on camera) – mirror and mirror-bearers disappear. There is a ripple and a turbulence in the water that indicates their passing . . .

After the slightest suggestion of an eddy of khaki-coloured mud and a black-grey smudge of soot . . . the water clears.

11.6 Medium shot. Prospero – sitting on his chair – watches as the small yellow ship drives forward towards Ariel's stream of crystal-clear water . . . the ship rocks and bucks on the rough, choppy water.

11.7 Ariel stands on the poolside – with a smiling, laughing face, his head thrown back, his hands on his hips . . . the water glistening and flickering from below onto his face and body – an image of exhibitionist impudence.

THIS PLATFORM WRITING-ROOM OF DA
MESSINA'S ST JEROME WITH ITS SHELVES,
STEPS, SLOPING DESK AND POT-PLANTS,
WAS A MODEL FOR PROSPERO'S 'POOR CELL'.

SECTION 12
PROSPERO'S STUDY

12.1 Now, for the first time, we can see the whole of Prospero's study or writing area. Lit by a mellow, orange-yellow light, is a writing room or study. It is based on the writing-study in da Messina's painting of 'The Study of St Jerome'. It could in fact be anywhere . . . in a palace, seminary, library . . . in a university or house in Italy, France, the Low Countries . . . maybe in England or Spain. Anywhere in fact in early seventeenth-century Europe . . . anywhere, in fact, in 1611.

It is a wooden structure with a writing-desk . . . there are shelves, cupboards, pen-racks, a chair, a bench, a lectern, steps, space for plants, scientific instruments, specimens and hooks for hanging clothes. It is a structure which can be dismantled and reconstructed – sometimes with other parts . . . sometimes in a different arrangement. When dismantled, it is portable and can be assembled anywhere . . . on the beach, in a forest, among rocks, on board a ship, beside a volcano. It is the property of Prospero, formerly 4th Duke of Milan, now living as an exile on an island far from Italy. It is a piece of civilised Europe transported to an island far from the sophisticated centre of things . . . perhaps off the north-west coast of Africa . . . maybe further down the African coast . . . perhaps further out still in the Atlantic Ocean. It is the study or writing room where Prospero thinks and reads, speculates and ruminates and dreams – and, on occasion – sleeps. Prospero has always felt most at ease in a study, surrounded by books. It is a place where he can think most readily of his past and contemplate most pertinently what is left of his future. It is the place where Prospero would plan a revenge on his enemies.

There is much evidence in the writing room of Prospero's preoccupations. He is not a necromancer, though there is evidence of a curiosity about alchemy and astrology. He is not wholly a closeted academic, for there is much which demonstrates his interest in the contemporary world. He has the enquiring, scholastic imagination which recognised no boundary between art and science or literature and natural history and, open-minded and unprejudiced, looked forward to the first century of science – the seventeenth. He is a master-enquirer like a da Vinci – even more like his (almost) contemporary Athanasius Kircher, scientist and humanist, whose enquiry covered every aspect of knowledge – the architecture of the Tower of Babel, the construction of the Ark, the exploration of China, manipulative acoustics, linguistics, seismology, medicine, magic, resurrection, Islam, the education of children, Egyptian hieroglyphics and much else. Books by this poly-glot and polymath were written and published nearly annually and were eagerly awaited and bought by the libraries of Europe. Kircher himself was like a book-making machine . . . and, for his time, his volumes were full of erudition, imaginative speculation and good sense. In this film, Prospero is like a Kircher book-making machine . . . turning books into more books . . . though his audience can only be himself.

In pride of place in Prospero's writing-study – are his original twenty-four books – the twenty-four books that Gonzalo threw into the leaky vessel that took Prospero and Miranda from Milan into exile. There is an ingeniously made brass-and-wood bookcase – with flaps and sliding panels, hinged drawers, rotating turntables . . . which has been made for the books – a bookcase with twenty-four differently-sized compartments – each compartment exactly tailored for each book. Some of the books are obviously thick and squat, some tall and thin, some huge and bulky. For the moment . . . at least half of the twenty-four books are missing . . . their respective compartments are empty. We have seen two of these books already – *The Book of Water* (in the bath-house) and *The Book of Mirrors*. By the time this film ends we will have made the acquaintance of each of the twenty-four books . . . and sometimes in the most unexpected places. The book that Prospero is writing – *The Tempest* itself – will be the twenty-fifth. Maybe there is – already waiting in expectation – a twenty-fifth compartment in the special bookcase.

12.2   In medium close-up, speaking at the same time as he writes . . . Prospero continues to play the parts of all the mariners . . .

PROSPERO:
Use your authority. If you cannot, give thanks you have lived so long, and make yourself ready in your cabin for the mischance of the hour, if it so hap.

12.3   In close-up we see what he has written 'Cheerly, good hearts . . .' After we have seen what he has written, the camera travels down the book to see – lying on it – the open pages of *The Book of Mirrors* . . . and reflected in it the same image as before – the drenched ship's company.

SECTION 13
THE BATH-HOUSE

13.1   Prospero – in the bath-house – is confronted by the mirror-image again.

Mirror-image: Two drenched, dark-skinned minions hold up a mirror (a smaller mirror than last time). In it is reflected the same image (now cropped in the smaller mirror) of the water-sodden ship's crew – but standing forward of the rest is the boatswain, dressed in oilskins in the driving rain with a heavy coiled ship's-rope around his shoulders. He is gesticulating in the storm.

The naked Prospero smiles and – in a whisper rising to a shout – he finishes the sentence we saw written on the page . . .

PROSPERO:
(Cheerly, good hearts!) . . . Out of our way, I say!

He then plunges his foot into the water with a mighty splash.

13.2   The water mercilessly rocks the small boat.
13.3   Prospero takes his clothes from the table and begins to dress. He covers his nakedness with a white linen under-robe.

PROSPERO (playing Gonzalo):
I have great comfort from this fellow. Methinks he hath no drowning mark upon him. His complexion is perfect gallows. Stand fast, good fate, to his hanging.

Prospero then puts on a second garment – a cream tunic embroidered in white – with a long row of small cloth-covered buttons down the front.

13.4   The smiling Ariel – hands on his hips, legs together – still sends an arc of water into the pool – but now he hovers slightly above the edge of the bath-side – his body tilted outwards over the water – like the figure on a ship's prow.

13.5   Prospero picks up his black, beaded cloak from the table . . . and as he puts it on – it magically begins to turn dark blue. He plays with the tas-selled cords that are part of the garment . . . and continues to speak the part of Gonzalo, amused at his own playing.

PROSPERO (playing Gonzalo):
Make the rope of his destiny our cable, for our own doth little advantage. If he be not born to be hanged, our case is miserable.

The mirror-bearers and their mirror disappear (using a locked-on camera, or they squat and dis-appear under the water).
Prospero – with a quick, almost impatient gesture – ties the cords of the cloak. He is now dressed – (his legs, feet and head are still bare). No longer is he a benign and slightly mischievous old man – but a figure of some wisdom. His smiling whispers and his mock amusement become serious – his con-jured storm is becoming a reality – his voice begins to boom around the stone spaces of the bath-halls.

PROSPERO (playing the Boatswain, in full voice):
Down with the topmast! Lower, lower! Bring her to try with main-course.

13.6 A wide perspective of the bath-hall. There is shouting and distressed howling deep among the columns. The light begins to dramatically darken further – lights swing and bounce.

13.7 Prospero slowly climbs the shallow steps out of the bath. He is rapidly becoming a figure of majesty and awe – no longer a vulnerable mortal. His cloak is now a lighter blue and is swiftly turn-ing purple.

13.8 Ariel has risen further above the waters of the bath and his body is gradually becoming more horizontal.

13.9 Prospero stands at the top of the stairs. His cloak is now dark red . . . and it is larger and more voluminous.

13.10 A close-up of Ariel's face . . . his smile is changing into an expression of grimness which looks particularly disturbing on one so young.

13.11 Prospero's cloak is now flaming crimson and is billowing in contrary winds . . . there is

movement beneath it as though it is alive with animals. A peacock and a voluptuous, naked water-siren dart out from its folds.

13.12 A close-up of the diminutive galleon tossed on the choppy water of the bath.

13.13 With renewed thunder desperate cries go up from the ship's company . . . Prospero's cloak is now a fiery red and has suddenly become five times as large. It is swathed and gowned about him like a regal curtain – reaching down to the water and held up behind him by swirls of wind and ten naked putti.
The world is in his cloak – figures peer out of its folds – mythological figures and snakes and pigs and flowers, naked fauns and heavy-breasted sirens and horses' heads – they sprawl on the flag-stones at his feet and peep out from under his arms . . . they are like the mythological world captured in the folds of a fallen marquee – a bacchanalian bed of rippling eiderdowns and frolicking figures intent on pleasure . . .
Four handsome, naked, female dancers separate themselves from the crowd in Prospero's cloak . . . and they dance. From now on – they become Pros-pero's dancers – they mark out a four-figured symmetrical space around him – dancing in per-fect unison – a strange, prancing, high-stepping, complicated, frankly sensuous dance – danced with great firmness and confidence – their erot-icism is only aimed at themselves – no mincing or quarter given – their erotic confidence is demon-strative and challenging.

PROSPERO (playing the Boatswain, in loud, resonating full-throatedness):
A plague upon this howling! They are louder than the weather or our office.

The noise of Prospero's magic has now reached its height. The noise of a thousand heavy, wooden fly-ing-machines bears down on us . . . coupled with the roar of wind and thunder, the braying of animals and the shouting and chattering of myth-ological figures, blown conches and the rush of water.

SECTION 14
THE BATH-HALLS

14.1 Echoic, grand chords of Prospero's magic-music crash in over the mechanical roar of his magic-sound-prelude which at once fades away . . . and Prospero turns and moves from the initial site of his creation of the storm in the bath-house . . . and, accompanied by his tumultuous music – walks among rows of parallel columns – through which – repeatedly – deep perspective vistas are revealed.

Here begins a three-to-four minute sequence to provide a background to the titles. Made up of travelling shots always moving from left to right following Prospero's walk – sometimes cutting ninety degrees across the action – by a sweeping camera or by editorial cuts . . . to pick up alternate angles and details in violent contrasts of light and dark and colour and shadow . . .

Prospero's progress through the columns perhaps invokes an elaborately-dressed papal figure striding quickly along Bernini's colonnaded arcades in St Peter's Square, where the square and side-streets are full of a packed host of Baroque theatrical acts and tableaux and processions – some of them subversive and carnal – put on for the edification and amusement of worshippers.

As Prospero purposefully walks forward, two ideas are being practised in the imagery – one to show the growth and wrath of the storm – the other to introduce the spirits and images and mythology of the island. On this occasion – the spirits impersonate classical and Old Testament mythologies associated with water . . . Moses – Leda – Neptune – a drowning Icarus – Europa – Jason – Hero and Leander – Noah . . . etc. – the watery images of a Renaissance imagination – mixing the sacred and the profane. There are also anachronistic images here – like references to Géricault's 'Raft of the *Medusa*' – (suitably Renaissance-ed) . . . because Prospero, as a magician, has foresight.

14.2 The columns, the stone floor, the coffered ceilings flicker with the lights of the approaching tempest. Now that Prospero has given life to the occupants of his ship . . . their voices ring out independently of him – echoing through the

WATER TO WATER. PROSPERO'S TEMPEST IS CONJURED IN HIS BATH-HOUSE WHICH REMAINS
AT THE EYE OF THE STORM TILL HIS ENEMIES ARE SHIP-WRECKED.

columned halls ... though they are in fact Prospero's voice much enlarged and echoed.

PROSPERO'S VOICE (playing the Boatswain):
Yet again! What do you here? Shall we give o'er and drown? Have you a mind to sink?
(playing Sebastian):
A pox o' your throat, you bawling, blasphemous, incharitable dog!
(playing the Boatswain):
Work you, then.

We can now understand something of the nature of Prospero's living quarters. His 'poor cell' is nothing of the kind, but is a – slightly forbidding – Piranesi palace – an architectural capriccio planned and invented and built by a man yearning for the classical architecture of Europe – of Renaissance Italy ... like the multiple styles of Hadrian's villa brought together through one organising imagination. The classical structures are built up and down a series of elevations - each separate area of the complex – though architecturally united – is arranged and decorated for a different function.

PROSPERO'S VOICE (playing Antonio):
Hang, cur! Hang, you whoreson, insolent noise-maker. We are less afraid to be drowned than thou art.

14.3 As Prospero walks through the columned corridors - his red cloak trailing and blowing like a sail – he is seen by the travelling camera from a low angle ... among the columns are glimpsed violent

images of a tempestuous sea – created by sudden moving projections of shadows that materialise into huge splashes of water . . . which at once retire – leaving the floor completely dry. There are court-yards among the columned buildings which are apparently open to the dark sky, for showers of rain hurtle into them like water poured from a bucket. Red lighting sticklebacks the columns. Black lightning. White lightning. Prospero walks through the storm unaffected.

PROSPERO'S VOICE (playing Gonzalo):
I'll warrant him for drowning, though the ship were no stronger than a nutshell, and as leaky as an unstanched wench.

14.4 Prospero walks among books that blow and rustle in the contrary winds. There are a great many of them . . . for Prospero's initial twenty-four books have begotten thousands more . . . they stand, lie and are piled high on stone tables and wooden desks and stone benches.

Covering the whole screen at one point is one very large book – maybe four metres by seven. It is open and slanted backwards like a raked stage. Sitting and crouching on the double spread of pages – with text and illustrations – are various mythological figures – Hades, the King of the Underworld, Vulcan, Juno and Venus . . . surrounded by lesser gods – Hercules and Ariadne accompanied by nymphs and putti who are endeavouring to turn the next huge page to free the occupants of the next chapter – fauns and hamadryads who are already struggling to get out. As if there were any doubt what this huge book is, its title is written across the top of each of the pages in the double-spread – *The Book of Mythologies*. This is the 'example-book', the template for Prospero's im-aginings to people the island. With this book – a primer and textbook of his humanist education – Prospero populates the island.

As Prospero walks on and leaves the screen on the right – the camera halts before the large *Book of Mythologies* – and the title of the film – *Prospero's Books* – is superimposed. As we watch, the nymphs and putti manage to turn the page – dislodging the former inhabitants and revealing others – this time mythological figures associated with water – Nep-tune and sea-goddesses, hamadryads, mermaids, sirens and mermen blowing conches.

All the time – before the noises of the approaching storm, Prospero's voice – playing the anguished mariners – continues to ring out.

PROSPERO'S VOICE (playing the Boatswain):
Lay her a-hold, a-hold! Set her two courses: off to sea again: lay her off.
(playing Mariners):
All lost! To prayers, to prayers! All lost!

14.5 The camera picks up Prospero again – he continues to walk among books which are now accompanied by all the known scientific instru-ments of the early 1600s – sextants and astrolabes, portable sun-dials, terrestrial globes, celestial globes, orreries.

PROSPERO'S VOICE (playing the Boatswain):
What, must our mouths be cold?

14.6 In among the columns – as Prospero walks through unheeding – we half-glimpse the curious, ambiguous creatures of the island – magically fashioned appropriate to Prospero's classical learning – all – at this moment – having some watery (often invented) connection. Lit by flashes of lightning – there are the original creatures of the island – some malign – the evidence of its black-magic past when Sycorax the witch was queen, and Prospero's power has not completely transformed them . . . and some benign – evidence of his new benevolent white magic. A naked elderly sea-siren – an oceanic Gorgon – with a lascivious, black-lipped smile and pendulous, empty breasts, an iri-descent tail and her hair infested with wriggling eels . . . squirms across a pile of books of fish.

14.7 . . . Persephone in a watery underworld . . . a naked, very white-fleshed, white-mask-faced, fleshy woman with blonde hair and large hips and an iron crown rusted with seawater and covered in black oil, holds a plate of burning spirit.

14.8   A young man – the drowning Icarus – covered in mud and entangled in ropes and huge, broken-feathered wings squirms and struggles in a puddle before a pile of open ornithological books.

14.9   In contrast to the mythological figures – the island has 'natives' fashioned here – perhaps related to Prospero's idea of the New World – as a group of American Indians - 'John White' Indians – with woad and string as clothing. They run laughing through an open space between the columns – shielding their heads from the tumultuous rain with pieces of bark.

14.10   A naked woman – hung up by her heels – hangs head down in a waterfall.

14.11   'John White' American Indians – three small children standing out in the downpour enjoying the crash of water on their bodies.

14.12   Neptune . . . an aged, naked male figure of the sea – sits darkly under a portico . . . with his young son at his feet . . . attended by sea-nereids leaning on his shoulders.

PROSPERO'S VOICE (playing Gonzalo):
The King and Prince at prayers! Let's assist them. For our case is theirs.
(playing Sebastian): *I'm out of patience.*

14.13   The three Graces – three very obese naked women with tattooed bodies – each standing in a bucket of water and admiring themselves in cracked mirrors.

14.14   Moses and Pharaoh's daughter: an 'Arabic-looking' female cradling a naked baby just taken from the water.

14.15   Leda . . . a long-haired girl playing with swans in a large bathtub surrounded by broken eggshells.

14.16   An oceanic bacchanal . . . tritons and nereids and small children with seaweed-hair sprawl in a dark puddle among maps and charts.

PROSPERO'S VOICE (playing Antonio):
We are merely cheated of our lives by drunkards:
This wide-chapped rascal – Would thou mightest lie drowning
The washing of ten tides!

14.17   A wind-blown fountain is filled with children who spit and spurt water at one another with water-filled cheeks.

PROSPERO'S VOICE (playing Gonzalo):
He'll be hanged yet,
Though every drop of water swear against it,
And gape at wid'st to glut him.

14.18   In a shiny wet chamber – a group of Olympian figures clamber and splash on a raft (*The Medusa*).

SECTION 15
THE BATH-HOUSE

15.1   Back in the bath-house . . . on the wooden table that stands in the shallow bath . . . the pages of *The Book of Water* are now blowing furiously in contrary winds . . . and then they blow violently shut. The continuous single drip from the high ceiling has been rapidly joined by other drops – falling percussively on different objects – basins, bottles, dishes . . . all with different resonances. Soon – and quite rapidly – it rains heavily across the whole of the bath.

15.2   Unaffected by the heavy rain . . . Ariel is now almost horizontally floating over the bath-house pool . . . and the diminutive ship is sucked into the choppy water where his stream of clear urine hits the pool. Then . . . the ship goes under.

PROSPERO'S VOICE (playing the Mariners):
Mercy on us!
We split, we split!
Farewell, my wife and children! Farewell, brother!
We split, we split, we split!

15.3   There is a loud flash and a mighty rumble and Ariel has gone . . . the lion leaps away . . . and a brilliant, blinding white light explodes – like a mammoth magnesium flare . . . flooding every inch of the screen into rasping over-exposure. The light – a star of Providence that Prospero himself creates – rises – slowly at first – with a great rumble and a mighty hiss of steam –

out of the water of the pool. It ascends with gathering speed – throwing dramatic black shadows behind the pillars and columns – right to the architectural horizon. Prospero's star rises up and disappears – trailing smoke and steam ... leaving behind – in the pool – momentarily – a hundred naked, squirming bodies – half-animal, half-human – churning the water into bloody mud. The rain now thunders down onto the pool.

PROSPERO'S VOICE (playing Antonio):
Let's all sink with the King!

Prospero's voice is now a mighty shout that rattles through the columns and echoes into the far distance.
The 'magic' music comes to an abrupt end.

SECTION 16
PROSPERO'S STUDY
(THE LAURENZIANA LIBRARY)
16.1 With the noise of the storm continuing (at a distance) – the words 'We split, we split, we split!' are seen written in Prospero's large book on his desk in his study or writing room.
16.2 Prospero – dressed in his flaming-red cloak – bent over his book – is suddenly aroused by the sound of large doors opening with a bang and a storm of wind rushing forth ...
the books and papers on his desk fly up into the air ...

AT THE CENTRE OF PROSPERO'S ISLAND PALACE OF LIBRARIES IS AN EXACT COPY OF THIS MICHELANGELO ARCHITECTURAL MASTERPIECE IN FLORENCE.

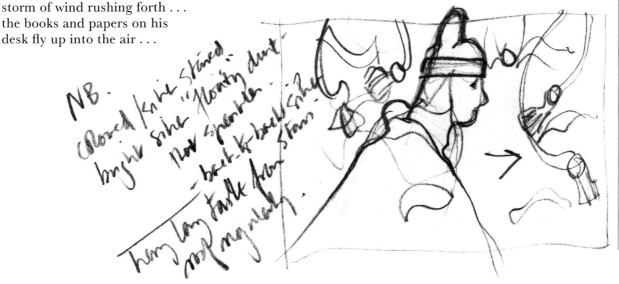

59

PROSPERO WALKS THROUGH A STORM OF FALLING PAPERS IN HIS LIBRARY BLOWN BY THE WEST WIND, A QUOTATION FROM BOTTICELLI'S BIRTH OF VENUS.

16.3 The air is full of swirling papers.

16.4 Prospero looks up . . . and we realise that his study or writing room is situated in a large, long, rectangular library . . . a library constructed to look like a facsimile copy of Michelangelo's Laurenziana Library in Florence.

16.5 The storm winds have been let into the library by the person of Prospero himself – who now strides into the space of swirling papers . . . we now have two Prosperos . . . the Prospero – dressed in blue – sitting at the desk who has dreamt up the scenario . . . and the Prospero as actor in his own drama – also dressed in red – walking past.

Whilst the Prospero at the writing-desk watches the Prospero as actor . . . the Prospero – as actor – is oblivious of the other's presence.

16.6 Prospero – as actor – walks down the length of the library among the cascading, flying, hurtling books, maps, charts and papers.

16.7 In the hurling, swirling storm of papers, naked mythological figures representing the winds stand on tables – they are grouped in pairs – a pair for each of the four winds – North, South, East, West – they stand, kneel, crouch on the tables among the scattered books – their cheeks puffed out – clutching one another for support – their hair streaming (Botticelli's 'Birth of Venus').

16.8 Lightning flickers at the rain-washed windows of the library.

16.9 Watched by the seated Prospero, Prospero the actor – unperturbed – walks through the mêlée. Down the centre of the library are stacks of heavy books arranged in huge cubes, pyramids and hexagons. With careful deliberation – and from various parts of the library – Prospero selects some dozen or so volumes from the shelves.

16.10 The last book he selects is a book of navigation - he picks it up from a pile of astronomical works.

It is called *A Primer of the Small Stars*. It is bound in old black leather and has been much scuffed and rubbed – slipping into and out of countless tight pockets – for it is a pocket-book, 20 by 15 centimetres and about 2 centimetres thick. Prospero fondly reminds himself of its contents . . . when he opens it – it is surprising that it holds so much . . . so many folded maps tumble out . . . unfolding and unfolding . . .

16.11 Close-ups of the riffled and tumbled pages of *A Primer of the Small Stars* show –

(1) Flickering dark-indigo coloured maps lit up with dashing points of light and flaring comets.

(2) Brightly winking constellations flickering and shifting.

(3) Meteors flying out of its pages like bouncing spits of water on a hotplate.

(4) Minute globes and orbs – like drops of restless mercury – dashing across its pages.

(5) The moods of the dark night skies are variously represented like soft black velvet, like the shining black of a scarab beetle, like the patina-ed surface of Indian-inked paper, soft blotting-paper soaked in dark blue ink for forty days, like a black cat's fur shining in moonlight . . .

16.12 As Prospero looks at his book – his face is lit up by bright sparks.

16.13 Prospero walks on through the storm of papers in his library.

SECTION 17
THE LAURENZIANA LIBRARY ATRIUM

17.1 Prospero leaves the library and enters the library atrium, which exactly resembles in scale and detailing the Michelangelo atrium of the Laurenziana Library in Florence. Here the air is perfectly still – but the noise of the storm continues everywhere else.

17.2 Carrying his selected books . . . Prospero descends the shallow staircase and enters Miranda's bedroom.

THESE BOTTICELLI WINDS BLOW THE TEMPEST INTO PROSPERO'S LIBRARY TO TUMBLE HIS BOOKS AND SCATTER HIS MANUSCRIPTS.

ACT I SCENE II
SECTION 18
MIRANDA'S BEDROOM

18.1   Prospero walks into an area of columns designated as Miranda's bedroom. There are chairs and low tables, billowing curtains, books.

18.2   Miranda is asleep in bed – fifteen years old. She is moving around on her bed in the throes of a disturbing dream.

18.3   Prospero sits on a chair – a draped Savonarola – at the foot of her bed – *A Primer of the Small Stars* open on his knees – its black pages flickering with white stars. He sits very still, brooding – like a Blake/Fuseli figure – a dark Sybil or an ancient classical Titan.

18.4   Close-up of the book. Whilst stars still twinkle in its pages, and comets circle and meteors flash – we can see small but bright crimson numbers written in fine spidery handwriting – of six and nine digits in length – that flicker furiously . . . and thin dull red lines pulsate slightly – with sudden, bright red, dotted-line trajectories arcing across dark spaces.

18.5   The lighting and the storm still thrash about – blowing the curtains of Miranda's bedroom like ship's sails, rolling bottles across the floor, whipping the tassels and cords of the bedroom upholstery like the ropes and tackle blown against a ship's mast.

18.6   As we watch Miranda, Prospero plays her voice – not in a female or a falsetto voice, but in his own – but made innocent, tender and anxious.

PROSPERO (playing Miranda):
If by your Art, my dearest father, you have
Put the wild waters in this roar, allay them.
The sky, it seems, would pour down stinking pitch,
But that the sea, mounting to the welkin's cheek,
Dashes the fire out. Oh, I have suffered
With those that I saw suffer! A brave vessel
Who had, no doubt, some noble creature in her,
Dashed all to pieces.

18.7   *Mirror-image:* The curtains at the back of Miranda's bed part and two soaked, white-skinned nereids carry in an elegant mirror befitting the bedroom – it has a green/turquoise wooden frame carved with coiled shells picked out in gold. It shows . . . first the brooding Prospero . . . then changes an angle to see . . . underwater . . . the small yellow ship slowly sinking in dark water – in slow-motion – twisting and turning. Surrounding it – dwarfing it in scale – ambiguously seen – huge and handsome sea-sirens – with bleached hair on their heads and bellies – like Rubens nereids in the 'Marie de Medici' series. They float and swim – prodding the boat with their fingers.

SECTION 19
THE BATH-HOUSE

19.1   In the now darkened bath-house – a torrent of white rain lashes down – and amongst the vistas of columns beyond – the storm rages – flashing light in far, deep perspectives. High winds ruffle and blow the surface of the water in the bath – lapping against the wooden table and the chair – blowing the soaked pages of *The Book of Water* on its lectern.

Booming out in something like despair – is Gonzalo's speech – spoken by Prospero.

PROSPERO'S VOICE (playing Gonzalo):
Now would I give a thousand furlongs of sea for an acre of barren ground, long heath, broom, furze, anything. The wills above be done! But I would fain die a dry death.

SECTION 20
PROSPERO'S STUDY

20.1 In the large book on Prospero's desk . . . are the words: 'The wills above be done! But I would fain die a dry death.'
The ink is still wet and shining on the words 'dry death'. As we watch – the ink dries.

SECTION 21
MIRANDA'S BEDROOM

21.1 Miranda tosses in her bed.

PROSPERO (playing Miranda):
Oh, the cry did knock
Against my very heart! Poor souls, they perished.

21.2 *Mirror-image:* In Prospero's mirror – underwater – in slow-motion – ten or more naked male figures turn and tumble in rough water. The naked sea-sirens – now somewhat like Miranda herself –

try to catch them, support them and attempt to carry them back to the surface.

PROSPERO (playing Miranda):
Had I been any god of power, I would
Have sunk the sea within the earth, or ere
It should the good ship so have swallowed, and
The fraughting souls within her.

21.3 Prospero reaches out of his chair and gently touches Miranda's foot.

PROSPERO:
Be collected.
No more amazement. Tell your piteous heart
There's no harm done. No harm.
I have done nothing but in care of thee –
Of thee, my dear one: thee, my daughter – who
Art ignorant of what thou art: nought knowing
Of whence I am, nor that I am more better
Than Prospero, master of a full poor cell,
And thy no greater father.

PROSPERO'S CLOAK IS SCARLET WHEN WORKING MAGIC AND BLACK WHEN AT REST AS HERE, A COUNTERPANE FOR THE FRIGHTENED MIRANDA.

21.4   Prospero gently touches Miranda's hand and lays it on the folds of his magic cloak.

PROSPERO:
'Tis time
I should inform thee further. Lend thy hand,
And pluck my magic garment from me – So.

Prospero gently slides his cloak from his shoulders – without further disturbing her. He lays it in her arms. Its redness begins to fade into blue. Miranda turns in her sleep and wraps herself in the cloak. The magic is allayed, stilled and pacified . . . to Miranda the cloak is just her father's coat – like a large, familiar dressing-gown that is impregnated with the protecting smells of her father. The blueness of the cloak darkens. It comforts her – its magic quietens to pacify and protect her – all the qualities that Prospero would want of his cloak and his magic – to protect his most precious possession – his daughter. The blueness of the cloak darkens into black. The storm at once begins to abate.

PROSPERO:
Lie there, my Art.

SECTION 22
PROSPERO'S LIBRARY

22.1   By an act of magic – by reversing the film – the mêlée of papers strewn by the tempest across Prospero's library – all return to their rightful place. When they have returned – there is suddenly a black-out that affects all the windows along one side – some huge object has jammed itself right up against the windows – it is the shipwrecked vessel belonging to Alonso, the King of Naples. We dimly perceive the ship's timbered side – yellow – exactly like the model galleon we have seen.

22.2   In compensation for the loss of light – Prospero – in his black cloak – as author – sitting at his writing-desk in the middle of the library – lights a candle . . . at which moment some three or four

hundred candles light up around the library – making a soft yellow gloom against the obstructed daylight.

SECTION 23
MIRANDA'S BEDROOM

23.1   Miranda – clutching her father's – now black – magic cloak, turns over in her sleep and her body visibly relaxes. There are tears on her closed eyelids.

PROSPERO:
Wipe thou thine eyes. Have comfort.
The direful spectacle of the wrack, which touched
The very virtue of compassion in thee,
I have with such provision in mine Art . . .

SECTION 24
THE BATH-HOUSE

24.1   In the bath-house . . . the storm is rapidly stilled – the pavements dry, the dampness evaporates. The bath rapidly empties before our eyes.

24.2   Revealed on the bottom of the bath – exactly in its centre – on a small drift of yellow sand . . . is a composed still-life – the yellow model boat – still fully rigged and unharmed . . . the exotic collection of seashells that were originally placed on the wooden table . . . and *The Book of Water* – open at the page of the drawings of the diminutive galleon.

24.3   A close-up of the drawing of the diminutive galleon in *The Book of Water* – around it – arrows and figures move and flash – indicative of the rolling motion of the sea and the direction of the winds. As we watch – these figures slow their motion and finally are stilled.

PROSPERO:
. . . So safely ordered, that there is no soul –
No, not so much perdition as an hair,
Betid to any creature in the vessel
Which thou heard'st cry, which thou saw'st sink.

24.4 A wide shot. The lion that previously lay on the bath-side – walking between the drying puddles on the flagged pavements – returns . . . and stretches . . . and – in a new shaft of warm light – like warm moonlight – rolls on its back on a patch of now bone-dry pavement. A few drips of rain-water splash on the marble flagstones.

SECTION 25
MIRANDA'S BEDROOM
25.1 In Miranda's bedroom – slowly, the darkness of the storm begins to lift. Prospero ruminatively watches Miranda's face in sleep. The thunder dies far away.

PROSPERO:
Thou must now know further.

25.2 Prospero continues to watch Miranda. The sound of the torrential rain outside is receding. A songbird begins to hesitantly whistle after the rain. Behind Prospero's head – drips of water from the eaves drop past the window – they are back-lit by a warm after-storm light.

SECTION 26
PROSPERO'S STUDY
26.1 In Prospero's study – in the open pages of the large book propped up on his desk – Prospero has written the words: 'Thou must now know further.' The wet ink dries.

SECTION 27
THE FORMAL GARDEN
27.1 There is a formal garden running below Miranda's bedroom window – a garden like those Prospero might have known in Milan – full of small paths, steps, flowering shrubs, aromatic trees and a great many pots full of scented jasmine, plumbago, box, privet. This garden is more than an early seventeenth-century garden – it has ponds and fountains – more like the gardens of the Alhambra in Granada. The garden is sodden from the storm . . . and dark – lit by cool, white light.

27.2 In the half-dark – among shining tiles – water rushes along roof-gutters.

27.3 Water gushes from a water-spout. The songbird whistles with more confidence.

27.4 Water runs along the stems and leaves of tall grasses. A nightingale whistles.

27.5 Water splashes from leaves.

27.6 Against a black background – water-droplets form at the tip of a leaf and slowly drop into darkness.

SECTION 28
MIRANDA'S BEDROOM
28.1 In Miranda's bedroom, Prospero – staring at Miranda – plays her response.

PROSPERO (playing Miranda):
You have often
Begun to tell me what I am, but stopped,
And left me to a bootless inquisition,
Concluding, 'Stay: not yet.'

SECTION 29
THE FORMAL GARDEN
29.1 In the garden below Miranda's bedroom – where the trees and shrubs are sodden – but are now beginning to shine from the torrential rain – four naked young women and a small, naked three-year-old female child – a group of the island's 'John White' Indians – look out from their shelter under a clipped box-hedge. As befits the European imagination of Prospero – they have the look both of classical figures and of John White's American Indians.

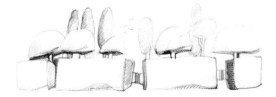

JOHN WHITE, ENGLISH DRAUGHTSMAN,
PAINTED THESE INDIANS IN VIRGINIA ABOUT
THE TIME SHAKESPEARE WAS WRITING.
THE ENGRAVER HAS CLASSICISED THEM
TO MASSAGE EUROPEAN TASTE, PRETTIFYING
THEM AND ADDING MORE THAN A DEGREE
OF EUROPEAN SEXUAL TITILATION.

SECTION 30
MIRANDA'S BEDROOM
30.1 Beside Miranda's bed.

PROSPERO:
The hour's now come;
The very minute bids thee ope thine ear;
Obey, and be attentive.

SECTION 31
THE FORMAL GARDEN
31.1 In the garden – the child – seeing the rain has stopped – takes a step out onto a gravel path and puts her foot experimentally into a puddle. Prospero's memory is prompted.

PROSPERO:
Canst thou remember
A time before we came unto this cell?
I do not think thou canst, for then thou wast not
Out three years old.

SECTION 32
MIRANDA'S BEDROOM
32.1 In Miranda's bedroom, Prospero stares at the sleeping Miranda.
As Prospero now relates his history – so the history is seen in images that move in a slow-motion that just takes the edge off natural action ... and in pale colours – as though Prospero was conjuring them in the air for Miranda to see as tableaux or paintings ... indeed there is the suggestion that – like the mirror-reflections we have already seen – the images are carried by mythological characters of Prospero's imagining – the happier images carried by putti and the darker images by leprous hags and disreputable fauns.
Whereas the mirror-images were very 'alive' – being spontaneous imaginings from Prospero's brain – these 'picture-images' are more controlled – in colour and composition – to correspond with a notion that they are images of long standing ruminated upon by a brooding Prospero. The images

recall the sumptuous paintings of Veronese but are framed and composed and cropped in a very modern manner – suggesting appropriately that we are not given the whole image – neither the whole happiness nor the whole perfidy.

32.2 *Mirror-image:* The images start with Miranda as a three-year-old – standing naked in a basin of warm water being bathed – it is the same child that stood in the wet garden. Her attendants are seen only in part – not their faces – only their hands and arms. They are in fact the same women we saw in the garden – now they are dressed in Italian aristocratic servant's clothes of around 1600.

PROSPERO (playing Miranda):
Had I not
Four or five women once, that tended me?

32.3 We now see the four or five women tending Miranda at her bath – more of the women's bodies are now revealed – though their faces are still cropped out of the picture.

PROSPERO:
Thou hadst, and more, Miranda. But how is it
That this lives in thy mind? What seest thou else
In the dark backward and abysm of time?

32.4 Musing – with his memory for hers – Prospero – looks up and stares back through the open door of Miranda's room, across the Laurenziana atrium into the library and beyond.

SECTION 33
THE COLUMNED CORRIDORS

33.1 The camera tracks off along the path of Prospero's gaze, gathering speed until it is travelling quite fast through the long perspectives of the columned corridors, as though searching for a reality conjured into being by Prospero's memory.

PROSPERO (voice-over):
If thou remember'st aught ere thou cam'st here,
How thou cam'st here, thou may'st.

Twelve year since, Miranda, twelve year since,
Thy father was the Duke of Milan, and
A prince of power.

33.2 The camera – in its wandering – approaches an animated 'painting' – mirror (painting) image – held by putti wearing helmets that are too large for them . . . and sashes that drag on the floor. The 'painting' introduces scenes of pomp . . . richly-dressed courtiers parade at a banquet in the style of Veronese. The characters are dressed in pale colours – pink, cream and white – the composition is cropped to show only shoulders, waists and gesturing hands.

A PANORAMA OF MEN AND ARCHITECTURE EMPLOYING THE GLITTER OF WORLDLY PLEASURE – FOR PROSPERO TO COPY WHEN ENTERTAINING THE WEALTHY NEAPOLITANS.

33.3 The camera moves around a columned corner to see more putti holding – in a pillared embrasure – a further 'animated painting' – mirror (painting) image – of a state bedroom Prospero's wife reclines on a sofa playing with the three-year-old Miranda who is naked from her bath. They are located in a welter of rich brocade and patterned fabric. Miranda's mother makes a single swift turn of the head and we catch sight of a woman in her

ANTONIO GATHERS HIS CONSPIRATORS AROUND HIM TO PREPARE FOR HIS COUP D'ETAT – A
PRETEXT TO SEE VERONESE THROUGH DUTCH EYES.

mid-thirties – a mature woman – the woman smiles – but the smile quickly fades.

PROSPERO:
Thy mother was a piece of virtue, and
She said thou wast my daughter; and thy father
Was Duke of Milan; and his only heir
And princess; no worse issued.

33.4 *Mirror (painting) image:* To remind us of the artificial nature of the 'painting' – a putto runs across the front, dragging a dog on a leash. In the 'painting' there is more Veronese pomp – now black and dark red – Antonio and his friends – in state rooms against blackness, are deep in conver-

sation – surrounded by documents and armour. We see their torsoes, arms, hands, and a young boy slumped asleep with his head resting on his folded arms and surrounded by a sea of maps and charts.

PROSPERO (voice-over):
My brother, and thy uncle, called Antonio –
I pray thee, mark me – that a brother should
Be so perfidious! – he whom, next thyself,
Of all the world I loved, and to him put
The manage of my state: as, at that time,
Through all the seigniories it was the first . . .

33.5 *Mirror (painting) image*: Acting as a 'wipe' and

as a distraction – a woman carrying a basket of flowers walks across the front of the 'painting'. In the 'painting' we see Prospero's well-appointed library in Milan – and travel across tables where scribes sit writing – surrounded by books, writing materials and scientific instruments.

PROSPERO (voice-over):
And Prospero the prime Duke, being so reputed
In dignity, and for the liberal arts
Without a parallel.

. . . The camera moves in through the mirror-frame and turns right to begin travelling along a library complex of bookcases . . . shelves of books all neatly ticketed and marked. We see three books in detail:

(1) *An Atlas Belonging to Orpheus.* The camera discovers a scribe gripping a piece of paper and a quill-pen in his mouth and resting the atlas on a pull-out lectern. The atlas is a huge book – some 60 by 90 centimetres and about 2 centimetres thick – and full of huge maps.

33.6   Medium shot. The scribe struggles to open the atlas on a landscape of Hell . . .

33.7   Close-up. There is boiling, sticky pitch . . . lines of blue and red fire . . . and streaks of black smoke . . . the pages are charred along their edges and perforated regularly in a squared pattern . . . out of each round perforation comes a puff of black smoke . . . it is a birds's-eye view of the middle-planes of Hell . . . a miniature rock-fall trails small stones and sand along the interior spine of the book . . .

33.8   . . . onto the floor of the library, where an assistant sweeps up the debris with a small brush.

33.9   (2) *A Harsh Book of Geometry.* An old man holding an abacus takes the book down from a high shelf, unwraps it from a leather case and opens it . . .

33.10   Close-up. Inside the book are hard line engravings of geometrical figures which, as the pages turn, rise up as three-dimensional forms – there is the sound of mechanical and metallic clanging as though the hard geometrical lines were thin metal rods. Small red and blue figures and letters flick over on the pages . . . fine, needle-thin pendulums swing – attracted by hidden magnets.

33.11   (3) *The Book of Colours.* Two young apprentice-scribes kneeling on the planked floor of the library . . . open a large red-covered book which immediately begins to flick over its own pages without human assistance. As the pages turn – so the colours move through gradual changes – the greens start with a deep blue-green and move through viridian, verdigris, emerald, turquoise – each page just a few degrees of colour different.

33.12   Close-up. The pages stay open on sea-green, and within its confines the image of a deep-green sea moves . . . one of the scribes dips his hand into the page and brings it out dripping with water and holding a wriggling eel . . .

33.13   A wide shot of the library reveals Prospero at the top of an arrangement of tables and seats and books where some forty or more jostling doctors, assistants and scribes surround him as they watch two surgeons dissect the body of a woman to discover the secrets of parturition. The camera pulls back to see the tableau as a painting or mirror-image supported on one side by a naked woman eating an apple and on the other by a naked woman singing, whilst at their feet children play with fruit and animals.

PROSPERO (voice-over):
Those being all my study,
The government I cast upon my brother,
And to my state grew stranger, being transported
And rapt in secret studies.

33.14   *Mirror-image:* Medium shot. A scribe, with bloodied fingertips – draws a bloodied foetus in a book full of medical drawings – it is a book we shall see later.

SECTION 34
MIRANDA'S BEDROOM

34.1   Prospero – deep in the contemplation of his history – pauses . . . and taking one of the heavier

VESALIUS, MASTER ANATOMIST FROM BRUGES,
DEALING 'IN SECRET STUDIES', PRODUCED
ANATOMICAL ENGRAVINGS WITHIN THE
TRADITION OF THE HEROIC HUMAN FIGURE.

volumes that he has on his knee – as he sits on the
Savonarola at the side of Miranda's bed – opens it
and places it on top of the *Small Primer of the Stars*. It
is Vesalius' *Anatomy of Birth* – a book of drawings
and diagrams of human anatomy.

34.2 . . . Beautiful drawings, but – as the pages
turn – terrible in their frankness – flayed bodies,
severed heads, trepanned skulls, depleted genita-
lia, dislocated bones . . . the drawings open up to
reveal more drawings underneath . . . most of all –

of images of procreation. As he turns the pages . . .
Prospeero's fingers appear to become covered in
blood . . . the organs of the body become three-
dimensional – small reproductions of the liver, the
spleen, the heart, the intestine . . . then red ink
floods the page . . . and then black ink. There is the
sound of babies crying . . .

34.3 . . . and then exultant singing . . . as Prospero – and we – contemplate a handsome and
awesome drawing of a woman giving birth . . . we
surmise that the woman is – was – Prospero's wife.
The diagram's discrete figures and dotted lines are
animated. Prospero's fingers enter the frame and
caress his wife's body.

34.4 A woman materialises behind Prospero –
leaning lightly on the back of his chair – she is
alternately a Titianesque nude and then the Vesalius figure – flayed – her blood vessels and nerve
endings and internal organs displayed and marked
with black figures and numbers as in the diagram
in the book . . . she leans lightly over and kisses
Prospero on the cheek. The kiss leaves a blood-red
mark on his withered cheek. Prospero shivers.

34.5 Four naked and whitened bodies – female
pall-bearers – looking suitably solemn – carry into
Miranda's bedroom a mirror draped in black.

34.6 *Mirror-image*: In the mirror we briefly see
Prospero's frightened reflection . . . and then as it
swiftly angles in the light – an image of Prospero's
wife – her white and naked corpse scattered with
yellow flowers – her hair elaborately braided – laid
out on a bier for burial.

34.7 Prospero muses . . . and looks down at the
book open on his lap . . .

PROSPERO:
Thy false uncle . . .

. . . and suddenly slams the book shut. The Vesalius woman standing behind his chair – vanishes.

PROSPERO:
Dost thou attend me?

Prospero suddenly – and angrily – shakes the
deeply sleeping Miranda . . . the books on his lap

crash to the floor . . . he then realises what he is doing and permits himself a wry smile.

34.8 Prospero moves a strand of hair from Miranda's face. He puts a hand on her shoulder . . . and then picks up the books from the floor and opens again the Vesalius *Anatomy of Birth* at the same drawing as before. He puts his hand on the drawing. He speaks very slowly.

PROSPERO:
Thy false uncle –
Being once perfected how to grant suits,
How to deny them, who t'advance, and who
To trash for over-topping, new created
The creatures that were mine, I say, or changed them,
Or else new formed them . . .

34.9 *Mirror-image:* The mirror-bearers hold aloft the mirror – the drapes have gone. Prospero dreams up again the image of wealth and military power that we have already seen in the mirror – Shot 33.4. The camera begins to move along some forty or more men – some standing, some sitting at tables, some swinging their legs as they sit on a bench . . . with dogs and drums, pikes and helmets, flags and small armaments – the image is cropped, so we only see the feet, legs and hips of men – some in armour – sitting at their tables – conferring on some plan or strategy – it is in fact the plot to remove Prospero from power.

In one quick, telling moment – we see a head – as a bearded and helmeted man bends to the floor to pick up a large dropped key . . . (a literal image for a symbolic one).

PROSPERO (voice-over):
. . . having both the key
Of officer and office, set all hearts i' the state
To what tune pleased his ear: that now he was
The ivy which had hid my princely trunk,
And sucked my verdure out of 't.

34.10 Prospero – now angrily wrapt in his history – takes some of his anger out on his

daughter – he shakes the sleeping Miranda again – like one who demands a wholly attentive audience to worry further over obsessional anxieties.

PROSPERO:
Thou attend'st not?
I pray thee, mark me.

Miranda stirs gently. Prospero takes his hand away.

34.11 Prospero stands up and begins to walk back and forth in front of the window of Miranda's bedroom. Through the window – the sky is clearing, but rainwater – back-lit now by bright sunlight – still steadily drips from the eaves.

There is the sound of a distant sea-horn – an optimistic sound – like an all-clear siren . . . and the sound of birdsong, and of water rushing in a small stream . . . and the distant sound of waves breaking on a beach.

PROSPERO:
I, thus neglecting wordly ends, all dedicated
To closeness and the bettering of my mind
With that which, but by being so retired,
O'er-prized all popular rate, in my false brother
Awaked an evil nature.

34.12 There follows a lengthy speech from an indignant Prospero which is intercut/interleaved/interwoven with the tracking shot we have already seen in the mirror . . .

Mirror (painting) image: In front of the travelling frieze of legs and feet and armaments and helmets and piles of documents . . . the three-year-old Miranda – dressed very formally in state clothes – playing with a lapdog and a small yellow model boat – the same yellow boat we have already seen . . . at her uncle Antonio's feet.

A male hand reaches down to stroke the girl's hair – whilst a female hand – her mother's – reaches down to take her small fingers and lead her away – they walk back along the line of legs and hips and feet – most of which are now more animated and have slightly changed their positions – Miranda disappears amongst them as

many stand and bow to let the small girl and her mother through their ranks . . .
The last evidence of their passing is the yellow boat pulled along on a string by the infant Miranda . . . the track ends on an indolent, foppish soldier lying full-length on the ground who doesn't get up – but makes half a lewd gesture towards Miranda's mother's skirts.

Prospero:
. . . And my trust,

34.13

Prospero:
Like a good parent, did beget of him
A falsehood in its contrary as great
As my trust was: which had indeed no limit,
A confidence sans bound. He being thus lorded,
Not only with what my revenue yielded,
But what my power might else exact, like one
Who having into truth, by telling of it,
Made such a sinner of his memory,
To credit his own lie, he did believe
He was indeed the Duke. Out o' the substitution,
And executing th'outward face of royalty,
With all prerogative – hence his ambition growing.
Dost thou hear?

34.14 Wide shot. Prospero breaks off – he now looks like a tired and weary – even cantankerous – old man. His hair is ruffled. His anger has made him mean – he knows it. He softens, and ruefully and a little ironically – puts words into Miranda's mouth.

Prospero (playing Miranda):
Your tale, sir, would cure deafness.

34.15 Close-up. He repeats the line for himself – ruminating on the enormity of the crime.

Prospero:
Your tale, sir, would cure deafness.

34.16 Prospero sits back in his chair. Behind him – the sky – through the wide window – is deep blue with large white clouds – with a solitary star defying the blueness. Cloud shadow flickers intermittently across the room. Prospero sits impassively like a doge. On his lap are his selected books. He cradles them.

Prospero:
To have no screen between this part he played,
And him he played it for, he needs will be
Absolute Milan.

34.17 The camera tracks back from Prospero as he walks his fingers across the covers of the books in his lap. When he opens their pages – his face is brightly lit from their magical glow.

Prospero:
Me. poor man, my library
Was dukedom large enough.

The camera continuing to track back . . . has revealed, on the left of the screen, the rear of a mirror carried or supported by mythological figures – elderly, battle-scarred, dignified, moustachioed, martial titans in half-armour. As the camera continues to track back, the mirror is swung around for us to see the reflected image within it. By the time the camera has stopped tracking back – Miranda and Prospero and Miranda's bedroom are completely hidden behind the mirror and the mirror-image covers the whole screen.
Mirror (painting) image: A grand political tableau of international diplomacy: Antonio standing – surrounded by flags and horses – over-politely pays homage to the seated King of Naples. Seven 'political' prisoners in rags and chains kneel at the

King of Naples's feet. It is an image that recalls Velásquez's 'Surrender of Breda'.

PROSPERO:
Of temporal royalties
He thinks me now incapable; confederates,
So dry he was for sway, wi' the King of Naples,
To give him annual tribute, do him homage,
Subject his coronet to his crown, and bend
The dukedom, yet unbowed –

34.18   A medium close-up of the 'political' prisoners in chains.

PROSPERO:
– alas, poor Milan!
To most ignoble stooping.

34.19   In Miranda's room – Prospero – indignantly – addresses his remarks to the sleeping Miranda.

PROSPERO:
Mark his condition, and th'event; then tell me
If this might be a brother.

He opens the Vesalius *Anatomy of Birth* on his lap.
34.20   ... at the page of the drawing of the woman in labour we have already seen

PROSPERO (playing Miranda):
I should sin
To think but nobly of my grandmother:
Good wombs have borne bad sons.

34.21   From a position behind Prospero – looking over his shoulder at the Vesalius book ... the camera begins to move away across the room to approach the mirror held by the martial titans and then 'move into' its image.
Mirror (painting) image: A night-time scene – lit by candles. In a large chamber – a Turkish bath-house – the same bath-house as Prospero owns and we have seen – but remade in Prospero's imagination as a place of malign intrigue – a lowered canvas ceiling stretched between the columns perhaps, and candles floating on the water ... with shadows and reflections flickering on the walls and

ceilings and a slow drift of steam. Antonio and Alonso – both naked for the bath – sit on the side of the bath by the remains of a large meal. Servants – male and female – depart to leave them in conference – the servants' departure, with a host of candles, leaves the two men illuminated in yellow and orange flickering light – isolated in the darkness. A dwarf-masseur with a head like a faun – watches them from a small upturned box on a table.

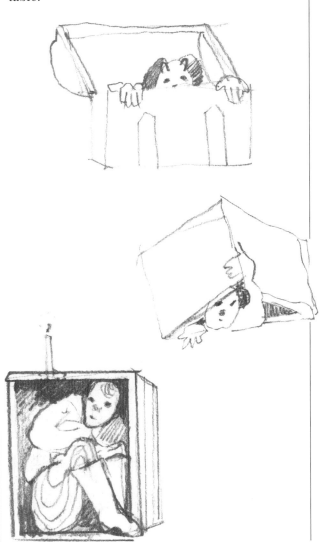

PROSPERO (voice-over):
Now the condition:
This King of Naples, being an enemy
To me inveterate, hearkens my brother's suit;
Which was, that he, in lieu o' the premises
Of homage, and I know not how much tribute,
Should presently extirpate me and mine
Out of the dukedom, and confer fair Milan,
With all the honours, on my brother.

34.22 *Mirror (painting) image:* In the darkened bath-house – Antonio smiles and, picking up a gold coin from a small pile by his side – throws it into the bath of still and steaming water . . . it splashes, and the ceiling of the dark bath-house – at once shimmers with reflected light . . . it is a signal. The smiling dwarf-masseur – his knees tucked up – leaps from his box into the water to retrieve the coin. The splash he makes rises in a back-lit shower of droplets.

34.23 *Mirror (painting) image:* A dramatic cut. A sudden, violent, crowded image of forty armour-clad legs and feet marching away from us – the camera follows very closely. The soldiers are framed from the thigh down – the noise of their armour, spurs and iron-clad feet on the stone flags is deafening. Huge gates are thrown open onto a wide ultramarine night sky – lit by a thousand stars and the roof-line of Milan. There is abrupt silence . . .

PROSPERO (voice-over):
Whereon,
A treacherous army levied, one midnight
Fated to the purpose, did Antonio open
The gates of Milan.

We wait – it seems for minutes – looking at the night sky. Then, suddenly breaking the silence and making us start with alarm and fear . . . there is a savage, heart-rending, gurgling scream.

34.24 *Mirror (painting) image:* The camera hurries through a ravaged library – ancient scribes bludgeoned – blood and ink in a blood-bath, books scattered.

34.25 *Mirror (painting) image:* The camera hurries through a ravaged dormitory – servants murdered in their beds with tall pikes stabbed into the corpses among the bloodied sheets.

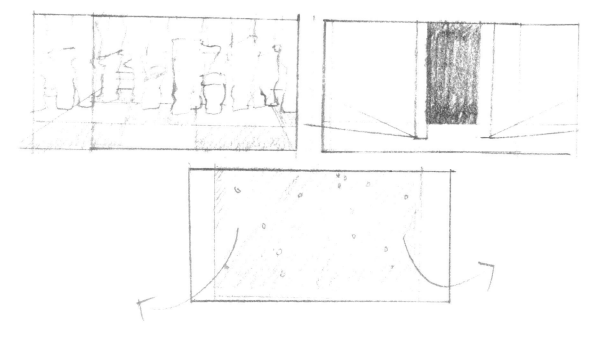

34 24. atrocities

34.26 *Mirror (painting) image:* A naked man in his sixties – asleep in bed on a hot, still night – it is Prospero – surrounded by half-opened books that he has been reading before falling asleep.

PROSPERO (voice-over):
. . . and, i'the dead of darkness
The ministers for the purpose hurried thence
Me, and thy crying self.

The sleeping man is suddenly and violently gagged with a strip of drugged linen. He is dragged from his bed. He struggles. His clothes are thrown at him – principal among them is an embroidered dressing-gown – his magic cloak. Two soldiers force him into it – struggling to get his arms into the sleeves. In the struggle a book slips slowly off a pile and as the camera cranes down to follow it – Prospero is dragged away across the floor . . .

34.27 Close-up. On the stone-flagged floor the book opens and its pages slowly turn . . . it is *The Alphabetical Inventory of the Dead* – a list of all who have died on earth in every part of the known world . . . a voice chants their names with a sonorous but rapid whispering monotone . . . the pages are old and dusty . . . watermarked with diagrams of graves and tombs and embellished with designs for monuments to the dead . . . a grand monumental mason's catalogue overwritten with a hundred million names. The hands of a hundred scribes write the names unceasingly . . . and small lamps – arranged symmetrically in a huge courtyard – constantly flick out . . . and are replaced. We hear the doleful scratching of a hundred pens and the deep tolling of bells. Black metallic spheres are rolled into a brass pot. When we have seen enough, a hand – Gonzalo's hand – reaches down and snatches the book away.

34.28 *Mirror (painting) image:* A naked, sleeping child – the infant Miranda – is lifted from her cradle by a weeping maid. She is bundled into a brocaded coat.

PROSPERO (playing Miranda):
Wherefore did they not
That hour destroy us?

34.29 *Mirror (painting) image:* Twenty men – six on horseback – hurrying over a wide moonlit beach kicking up dry sand – with Prospero bound to a saddle.

PROSPERO:
My tale provokes that question. They durst not,
So dear the love my people bore me: nor set
A mark so bloody on the business.

34.30 *Mirror (painting) image:* A book dropped, a maid slumped down on the sand – on her hands and knees – exhausted . . . the infant Miranda's brocaded coat held in her arms.

PROSPERO:
. . . But
With colours fairer painted their foul ends.

34.31 *Mirror (painting) image:* The infant Miranda carried brusquely underarm – not crying but wide-eyed with amazement . . . passed arm to arm – in the dark – across water – the water sparkling upwards in the moonlight.

PROSPERO:
In few, they hurried us aboard a bark,
Bore us some leagues to sea; where they prepared
A rotten carcass of a boat, not rigged,
Nor tackle, sail, nor mast; the very rats
Instinctively had quit it.

34.32 *The First Night at Sea:* A still boat in the moonlight on an open, flat sea . . . a hooded Prospero, a child lying cradled asleep on a pile of open books – her finger in her mouth, her sex evident . . .

PROSPERO:
There they hoist us,
To cry to the sea that roared to us; to sigh
To the winds, whose pity, sighing back again,
Did us but loving wrong.
(playing Miranda):
Alack, what trouble
Was I then to you!

34.33 *The Second Night at Sea:* By the light of a dull red dawn – with white stars still in the sky . . . the

in the pool.

women, ape-men, flaming moons, golden lakes, levitation, two-headed sheep, walking skeletons and so on.

There is a flapping turtle at the bottom of the boat.

PROSPERO:
Oh, a cherubin
Thou wast, that did preserve me. Thou didst smile,
Infused with a fortitude from heaven,
When I have decked the sea with drops full salt,
Under my burthen groaned: which raised in me
An undergoing stomach, to bear up
Against what should ensue.

34.34 *The Fifth Night at Sea:* A greenish phosphorescent light ripples up from the sea. There is no moon, but a great swathe of small stars stretch across the sky and are reflected in the still water. Miranda sleeps – cradled in books – her head askew in a paper hat made from pages torn from

infant Miranda is chewing a crust of bread and peering intently at the pictures in one of Prospero's books that dwarf her. It is a book called *Travellers' Tales* and is open at a drawing of unicorns – to presage the first 'miracle' described in Shot 77.1: 'Now I will believe that there are unicorns. Travellers ne'er did lie, though fools at home condemn 'em.'

Travellers' Tales is a book of real, imagined, apocryphal and impossible events, places, people and things – a book of the expected curios – bearded

34.34.

one of them. She looks grubby but healthy. There is now an empty turtle-shell in the boat – beside the fresh corpse of a large seabird. Prospero has opened a small black-bound book – *The Primer of the Small Stars* – the same one that we have seen him hold in Miranda's bedroom – he compares its maps with the sky above his head.

34.35 *The Primer of the Small Stars* . . . out of which spill large black, dark blue and indigo-coloured folded maps – they are full of marked stars and constellations that appear to flash and twinkle as they lie in the book.

34.36 Prospero – looking tired but excited by his examination of the stars – makes a decision on his calculations and sits firmly to the side of the boat to weight its drift – he throws his cloak over the edge – in slow-motion – into the water to act as a drag.

PROSPERO:
Some food we had, and some fresh water, that
A noble Neapolitan, Gonzalo,
Out of his charity, who being then appointed
Master of this design, did give us, with
Rich garments, linens, stuffs and necessaries,
Which since have steaded much.

34.37 *The Tenth Night at Sea:* A half-top-shot. Miranda and Prospero are peacefully asleep in their boat . . . wrapped around . . . and lying on . . . and embracing . . . and being embraced by . . . the twenty-four books that Gonzalo put into the boat.

The sea is calm and a deep green . . . we can see the bottom of the sea-bed . . . and the boat is surrounded by a shoal of a hundred thousand small, darting, silver fish.

PROSPERO (voice-over):
So, of his gentleness
Knowing I loved my books, he furnished me
From mine own library . . .

34.38 Close-up. Prospero and Miranda asleep in the boat embracing and being embraced by the twenty- four books.

PROSPERO:
. . . with volumes that
I prize above my dukedom.

SECTION 34A
PROSPERO'S STUDY

34A.1 In Prospero's study – an imposing, symmetrical shot – Prospero – as a man of letters – is seen surrounded by the books that have made him what he is. Half-open on his desk, resting on his lap, embraced by his left hand – the books glow.

SECTION 35
MIRANDA'S BEDROOM

35.1 Medium shot. Prospero stands and lays eleven books out on Miranda's bed – around her sleeping body. He keeps one book in his hand. He stares down at the sleeping Miranda encircled by the books.

PROSPERO:
Here in this island we arrived.

35.2 *Mirror-image:* The camera turns ninety degrees to see . . . in a mirror held at the back of Miranda's bed by shadowy figures . . . in a thick dawn mist, the boat has beached on a sandy promontory of an island . . . Prospero lifts the sleeping infant Miranda out of the boat and lays her on the sand. There is a cry and a yelp and much sudden demoniac screaming . . . dark, ambiguous figures cavort threateningly in the mist on the beach.

35.3   Hastily, Prospero picks up Miranda and encircles them both with his twelve books – just like the books around the sleeping Miranda. He takes one of the books – *The Book of the Earth* – whose pages are impregnated with the minerals, acids, alkalis, elements, gums, poisons, balms, aphrodisiacs, alcohols of the earth – and places it at the top of the circle – and opens it at a page of bright redness – a thick, impasto, crimson pigment is impregnated into the page.

35.4   Close-up. Prospero runs his thumbnail diagonally across the page – white sparks follow his thumb . . . then the page – and the book – ignite with a bright pink flame.

35.5   Prospero stands back and the flames shoot out of the book without consuming the pages. The flames light up the sand with a pale pink light and the dark, half-animal, half-human figures are held at bay – yelping and snarling . . .

35.6   A mélange of devils . . . their fangs and demonstrative private parts, swirling hair, hooves and horns illuminated by the pale pink light.

35.7   With the pink flames burning from *The Book of the Earth*, Prospero and Miranda (still clutching the *Travellers' Tales*) have fallen asleep on the beach surrounded by the books and their other meagre possessions . . . behind them – down the beach . . . the 'devils' smash up the rowing boat, hurling the pieces into the sea. As we watch – the sun quickly rises – dispelling the mists and with them – the 'devils' . . . only their grunts and snarls are heard.

35.8   *Mirror-image:* No frame. Prospero surveys the island . . . a rocky island of ruins – Roman ruins . . . running down to the beach and the sea . . . with a dark forest behind . . . stretching to the horizon. Prospero speaks slowly and carefully – with great deliberation and intent – and almost in a whisper . . . willing his words to be true.

PROSPERO:
Here
Have I, thy schoolmaster, made thee more profit

Than other princesses can, that have more time
For vainer hours, and tutors not so careful.
Know thus far forth.
By accident most strange, bountiful Fortune,
Now my dear lady, hath mine enemies
Brought to this shore.

35.9   *A montage:* Intercutting shots of the various architectural structures Prospero has devised for the island – the bath-house, the bath-halls, the colonnades, the garden, the pyramid lighthouse, the quincunx etc. . . . with the plans, elevations and paper models that rise from the pages of a book as Prospero opens it – page by page – operating like a magnificent pop-up book – each new building to be accompanied by triumphant music, for the book is called *Architecture and Other Music*. The montage structure is in three sections:

(1) A bare stretch of island – maybe with a ruin – tumbled columns, fallen triumphal arch, outcrops of rocks and trees . . . filmed perhaps in some likely 'Roman' archaeological site with an interesting light ambience – dawn, dusk after-dark . . .

(2) Prospero's *Book of Architecture and Other Music* – opened at a page from which rises a complex paper model of a splendid building or set of buildings – complete with light-effects – maybe people moving within it, a little smoke perhaps and low clouds among the tall towers, maybe a rush of pigeons . . . along with figures and measurements and calculations and drawn geometrical lines that move, get erased, change angle etc. . . .

(3) The prototype equivalent building as it has been erected on the island – constructed there by Prospero's magic.

There should be at least five magnificent 'pop-up' book constructions which can be devised according to how the architectural sets are found or built. There are many ways of 'cheating' the comparisons in the paper model to match the sets – but there should always be some salient feature that creates an obvious pictorial synchronicity. The purpose of the montage is to show how Prospero's magic – aided by the book *Architecture and Other*

Music – has created the island's present state and appearance . . . the fallen columns have been raised and multiplied, the gardens have been cultivated, the libraries built, level fields of golden corn stretch to the forest which has retreated . . . pyramids, obelisks, free-standing columns . . . rise above the corn. Prospero, through his magic, has created a little idealised Renaissance Milan on a wild island.

The final montage image shows a panoramic view of the island – over which glints a silver star . . . and beneath it – for the most part hidden by the large building of the library – rise the tall masts, pennants and rigging of a yellow galleon.

PROSPERO:
. . . by my prescience
I find my zenith doth depend upon
A most auspicious star, whose influence
If now I court not, but omit, my fortunes
Will ever after droop.

35.10   Prospero closes the magic book and puts it down on the bed to join the others that ring Miranda. He gently unclasps his magic cloak from the arms of Miranda . . . she stirs and settles . . . her body relaxing into the sheets and pillows.

PROSPERO:
Thou art inclined to sleep. 'Tis a good dulness,
And give it way. I know thou canst not choose.

Furling and unfurling the folds of his cloak – he magically produces the small model of the yellow galleon . . . and holds it up so that it catches the light of the silver star in the sky. He puts on the cloak – it turns blue. He leaves Miranda's bedroom – carrying the model ship – its light apparently making the surrounding daylight seem dark.

SECTION 36
THE LIBRARY ATRIUM
There now follows a sequence introducing Ariel and establishing him and his history.
As Prospero walks quickly back through the library and corridors and halls of his domain – on his return to the bath-house where the magic of this fateful storm was inaugurated – he speaks for Ariel. He continues to carry the model yellow ship before him like a bright lighted beacon in a darkness that surrounds him and his magic (now blue) cloak.

36.1   As Prospero walks through the echoic spaces of the Laurenziana Library atrium, he calls to Ariel.

PROSPERO:
Come away, servant, come! I am ready now.
Approach, my Ariel, come!

Prospero's voice – speaking for Ariel – acoustically swooping and darting and gliding and sweeping – answers echoically out of the walls and the columns and the air.

PROSPERO (speaking for Ariel):
All hail, great master! Grave sir, hail! I come
To answer thy best pleasure: be't to fly,
To swim, to dive into the fire, to ride
On the curled clouds, to thy strong bidding task
Ariel, and all his quality.

SECTION 37
THE LIBRARY
37.1   A virtuoso, bravura travelling shot to be accomplished in one take from end to end of the library – depicting the energetic bond between Ariel and Prospero and to show Prospero's powerhouse of magic – his library – the repository of his books and his power.
Prospero walks swiftly through the library . . . Ariel keeping pace with him by jumping and leaping from table to table down the length of the library. Ariel's naked body is blindingly white and is accompanied by a red and orange nimbus . . . often he seems to disappear as he lands on a book-strewn table – as though – one of his natural elements being air – he can best be seen only when he is flying.

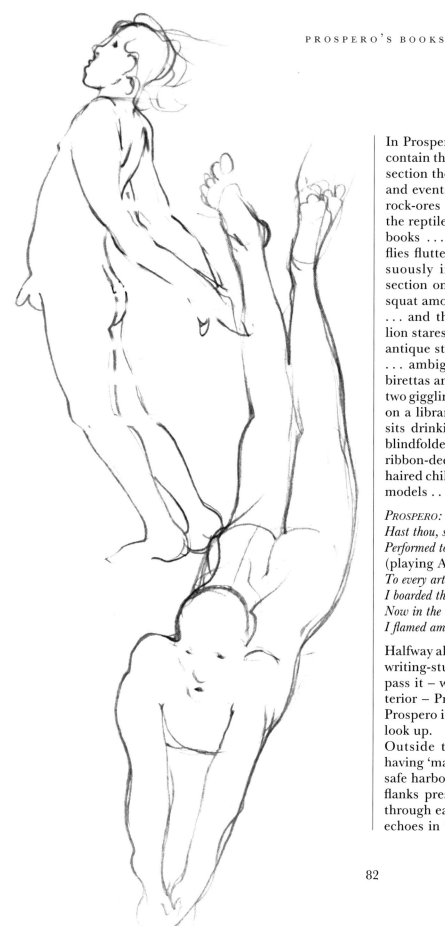

In Prospero's library – the books seem unable to contain their arcane knowledge, and at each book-section there is an overspill of objects and people and events ... in the mineral section – glittering rock-ores and brilliant coloured pigments ... on the reptile shelf – yellow snakes twine among the books ... bird-sized brilliantly-coloured butter-flies flutter in the entomological section ... sensuously intertwined nymphs lounge near the section on erotica ... small music-playing fauns squat among the music-score shelves.

... and there are ambiguous confusions ... the lion stares at Prospero's passing from a jumble of antique statuary and fractured stone inscriptions ... ambiguous bacchanalian figures – wearing birettas and mitres – sit astride a giant abacus ... two giggling nereids – playing with a sheep – swing on a library stepladder ... a long-tailed creature sits drinking in the shadow of a tall desk ... a blindfolded figure of pornography sits with a blue-ribbon-decorated fat pig in her lap ... a long-haired child sleeps coiled up among mathematical models ...

PROSPERO:
Hast thou, spirit,
Performed to point the tempest that I bade thee?
(playing Ariel):
To every article.
I boarded the King's ship. Now on the beak,
Now in the waist, the deck, in every cabin,
I flamed amazement.

Halfway along the library is Prospero's da Messina writing-study ... it is half-curtained, but as we pass it – we see inside in the yellow candlelit interior – Prospero, the writer, bent over his desk. Prospero in the da Messina writing room does not look up.

Outside the north library windows, Prospero having 'magicked' the full-size yellow galleon to a safe harbour – we see its yellow-boarded, curving flanks pressed close to the outside library walls through each successive window. As Ariel's voice echoes in the library so his descriptions of flame

82

and lightning are re-enacted as light-effects along the ships's flank – lighting up the windows and causing flashes of illumination to shine into the library, throwing the bookcases, the scientific instruments, the bacchanalian figures and Prospero himself into sharp relief and contrasting shadow – it is a re-enactment of the storm in light-effects.

PROSPERO (playing Ariel):
Sometime I'd divide,
And burn in many places: on the topmast,
The yards and bowsprit, would I flame distinctly,
Then meet and join. Jove's lightnings, the precursors
O' the dreadful thunder-claps, more momentary
And sight-outrunning were not.

When Prospero leaves the library – the camera swings ninety degrees as the elements of his library grow comatose . . . and return to their rightful places inside the books . . . after ten seconds the library is neat and organised . . . the various figures and objects and animals gone . . . the library tidy and well-disciplined . . . only the lights continue to flicker outside the north window along the flank of the yellow ship.

SECTION 38
THE BATH-HALLS
38.1   Prospero – through a cloud of sparks and mist – now enters the columned corridors and inclined passageways with shallow descending steps that lead down to the bath-house. Ariel is now absent (and we wonder where he is) . . . but Ariel's voice (played by Prospero) still conjures up the images of his fiery influences in the storm – red fire-splashes and bursts of white light that continue to flash and burn and sparkle amongst the columns and the long dark perspectives.

PROSPERO (playing Ariel):
The fire and cracks
Of sulphurous roaring the most mighty Neptune
Seemed to besiege, and make his bold waves tremble,
Yea, his dread trident shake.

38.2   In response to Ariel's description – deep in the shadowy spaces of the corridors – the sea-mythological creatures we saw before make their reappearances – especially the figure of the ancient, bearded Neptune waving his trident . . .

PROSPERO:
My brave spirit!
Who was so firm, so constant, that this coil
Would not infect his reason?
(playing Ariel):
Not a soul
But felt a fever of the mad, and played
Some tricks of desperation. All but mariners
Plunged in the foaming brine, and quit the vessel,
Then all afire with me.

38.3 There are glimpses of ambiguous, wet, bedraggled, naked figures – supported and attended by mythological creatures – wandering among the columns – including a dozen or so mortal figures seen clinging to a raft.

SECTION 39
THE BATH-HOUSE

39.1 Prospero enters the bath-hall where the film began. The bath-house is darkened – most of the light arising out of the still water in the shallow pool. A draught swirls around the bath-house – pulling at the thin, hanging drapes. Prospero walks to the edge of the shallow steps that descend into the pool.

Ariel's voice – still played by Prospero – echoes about him.

PROSPERO (playing Ariel):
The King's son, Ferdinand,
With hair up-staring – then like reeds, not hair –
Was the first man that leaped: cried . . .

39.2 The pool begins to swirl and bubble . . .

PROSPERO (playing Ariel):
'Hell is empty,
And all the devils are here.'

. . . and Ariel – on Ferdinand's last quoted cry – erupts upwards out of the pool in a mighty splash of water. Ariel's body is coloured and stained the colours of his recent magic – red and orange for flames, white and pink for the lightning . . . he hovers above the water – smiling and benign and impudent – the water running down his face, his chest, his belly . . . dripping off his body.

PROSPERO:
Why, that's my spirit!
But are they, Ariel, safe?

39.3 Apparently hiding under the water of the bath – six muscular sea-creatures rise up out of the water and carry with them a long and heavy rectangular mirror.

39.4 *Mirror-image*: In the mirror is a reflection of Ariel's (through Prospero's) imagining – an image that itself reprises the mirror-bearers' appearance out of the water. For . . . from a stretch of calm sea . . . appear eight male heads – wet and bemused . . . then their shoulders are revealed . . . then their chests and waists . . . and then . . . more men appear – sitting and kneeling . . . they have risen up through the waves as though on a subaquatic lift . . . for a moment it looks as though all twelve men are being supported on the surface of the sea . . . then the reason for their flotation is made plain – they are standing on a raft . . . of wooden, slatted boards – like the deck of a ship . . . the water sluices away through the slatted boards . . . and twelve bemused, naked, somnambulant figures stare at their predicament.

In a flash . . . out of the water appears a mythological brood – nereids, fauns, dryads . . . with towels, fine clothes, mirrors, combs . . . the shipwrecked survivors are dried, combed, dressed. They stand and preen – magnificent – with cartwheel ruffs of extreme circumference, with lace at the cuff and breast . . . wide sashes at the shoulder and waist – black and white and silver . . . with elaborate boots on high soles and heels – so high – they stand on stilts – shining with spurs and flashing with white and silver linings that spill extravagantly over the boot-tops . . .

PROSPERO (playing Ariel):
Not a hair perished;
On their sustaining garments not a blemish,
But fresher than before.

39.5 . . . the raft is guided ashore by the mythological company who wade and swim about its sides – the raft is beached and the company disembark onto the sand . . . the mythological company gambol in the surf and then disappear along with their wooden raft . . . the sea is calm and empty and sunlit to the horizon . . . the over-dressed courtiers stand bemused on the beach – incongruous in their finery, their urbane elegance, their effete splendour.

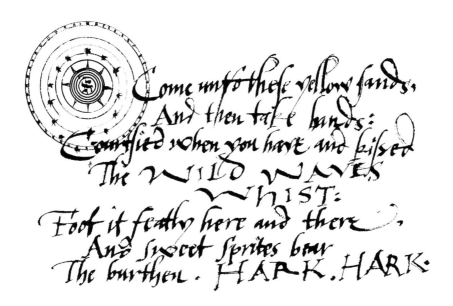

Whilst the raft is being guided to shore, the air is full of Ariel's song:

Come unto these yellow sands,
And then take hands.
Courtsied when you have, and kissed,
The wild waves whist,
Foot it featly here and there,
And sweet sprites, the burthen bear.

39.6 Ariel – in the bath-house – still hovering above the water – watches Prospero who is watching the mirror-bearers. They rest the mirror down in the water so that it reflects him, Prospero, standing by the pool-side.

PROSPERO (playing Ariel):
And, as thou badest me,
In troops I have dispersed them 'bout the isle.
The King's son have I landed by himself,
Whom I left cooling of the air with sighs
In an odd angle of the isle, and sitting,
His arms in this sad knot.

Ariel – floating in the air above the bath – folds his arms and his legs and rests a mock-melancholy head on his arms. The mirror-bearers, standing in the water, turn the mirror so that it reflects another angle of Ariel. The mirror-bearers and Prospero all fold their arms.

SECTION 39A
PROSPERO'S STUDY
39A.1 Prospero – seated in his study – has his arms folded in the pose indicated for Ferdinand by Ariel and by his 'double' Prospero in the bath-house. Looking towards the library windows beyond his wooden study where the yellow galleon has come to rest . . . Prospero unfolds his arms, takes up a pen and writes . . .
39A.2 Close-up of Prospero writing . . . 'Safely in harbour is the King's ship . . .'
Slowly the writing mixes into the next shot.

SECTION 40
THE BATH-HOUSE
40.1 *Mirror-image*: In the mirror held by the mirror-bearers standing in the water of the bath-house – we see – in the reflection – the interior of the yellow, shipwrecked galleon: it is a shadowy space – lit from without – through small windows . . . like the interior of a building by day when there is snow on the ground outside . . . the large cabin is full of sleeping sailors . . . sleeping haphazardly where the storm has tossed them – but peacefully . . . some fully clothed in gaberdines and sou'-westers, some wearing only sea-boots and pigtails, some lying like naked crusaders on their tomb-

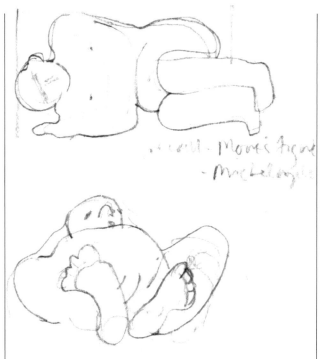

stones, or as though pleasantly exhausted after drinking or gluttony.

PROSPERO (playing Ariel):
Safely in harbour
Is the King's ship; in the deep nook where once
Thou call'dst me up at midnight to fetch dew
From the still-vexed Bermoothes, there she's hid:
The mariners all under hatches stowed;
Who, with a charm joined to their suffered labour,
I have left asleep.

40.2 Ariel hovers closer to the bath-pool . . . dragging his toes on the water-surface . . .

PROSPERO (playing Ariel):
And for the rest o' the fleet
Which I dispersed, they all have met again . . .

40.3 Ariel bends down, and with an outstretched finger, traces a diagram of the fleet's position on the surface of the pool . . . magically his marks remain – like chalk-marks on slate . . . or furrows in wet sand . . . or scratch-marks on ice.

PROSPERO (playing Ariel):
. . . And are upon the Mediterranean flote,
Bound sadly home for Naples,
Supposing that they saw the King's ship wracked,
And his great person perish.

40.4 Prospero – his face lit by the water-reflections from the pool – speaks to Ariel as Ariel relaxes – smiling – and cross-legged – sits down on the water-surface as though it was the ground. He leans back and lies out full-length on the water-surface, pillowing his head with his folded arms. All the while the red, orange and pink colour of his body fades back to the colour of pale flesh.

PROSPERO:
Ariel, thy charge
Exactly is performed: but there's more work.
The time 'twixt six and now
Must by us both be spent most preciously.

40.5 Ariel sits up on the water and begins to leap and bounce like a figure on a trampoline . . . the water just splashing a little where he touches it with his outstretched toes.

PROSPERO (playing Ariel):
Is there more toil? Since thou dost give me pains,
Let me remember thee what thou hast promised,
Which is not yet performed me – my liberty.

40.6 A stern Prospero stamps his feet and frowns with irritation.

PROSPERO:
Before the time be out? No more!

40.7 Ariel – in his agitation – now bounces and spins – like a figure repeatedly diving – in slow-motion – from a springboard.

PROSPERO (playing Ariel):
Remember, I have done thee worthy service;
Told thee no lies, made no mistakings, served
Without or grudge, or grumblings. Thou didst promise
To bate me a full year.

40.8 An even sterner Prospero.

PROSPERO:
Dost thou forget
From what a torment I did free thee?

40.9 Ariel – taking an even mightier spring – with guilty, impudent face.

PROSPERO (playing Ariel):
No.

40.10 Prospero's face – strongly lit from the water-reflections in the pool – is now swept with the shadow of sleet and snow. Behind him – against an ultramarine darkness – large white snowflakes drift quickly by.

PROSPERO:
Thou dost; and think'st it much to tread the ooze
Of the salt deep,
To run upon the sharp wind of the north,
To do me business in the veins o' the earth
When it is baked with frost.

40.11 Now high up in the air above the pool – twisting and turning – Ariel looks down on Prospero.

PROSPERO (playing Ariel):
I do not, sir.

40.12 Prospero – in a pose of anger that he enacts largely for Ariel's benefit.

PROSPERO:
Thou liest, malignant thing! Hast thou forgot
The foul witch Sycorax, who with age and envy
Was grown into a hoop? Hast thou forgot her?

40.13 Ariel – shamed into a more reasonably accurate version of the truth – begins to sink slowly out of the air towards the pool-surface.

PROSPERO:
Where was she born? Speak. Tell me.
I must once in a month recount what thou hast been,
Which thou forget'st.

40.14 Ariel's feet have touched the water-surface and he begins to sink under Prospero's invective – to his ankles . . . to his knees . . . to his hips . . . to his chest . . .

PROSPERO:
This damned witch, Sycorax
For mischiefs manifold, and sorceries terrible
To enter human hearing, from Argier,
Thou know'st, was banished. For one thing she did,
They would not take her life. Is not this true?

40.15 Ariel has now sunk to his throat – he looks shamefaced . . . a sad, disembodied, decapitated head resting on the water-surface.

PROSPERO:
This blear-eyed hag was hither brought with child,
And here was left by the sailors.

40.16 Prospero conjures an image in the reflecting mirror – now held not by muscular sea-creatures – but by crippled fauns and old hags.
Mirror-image: After a quick reflection of Prospero – the mirror is angled to reflect a night scene – with a moon – on a beach – surrounded by dwarfs, white horses and albino monkeys . . . where a rough palanquin – a bed with a canopy – four stakes tied with ribbons and the sides covered . . . is set down on moonlit sand by six sailors. Laughing – the sailors return to their rowing boat beached in the surf.

40.17 *Mirror-image:* Ariel is thrown from out of the drawn curtains of the palanquin. He is covered in blood and pus and excrement – his hair tied in a stupid knot like a lap-dog, his body tattooed and weighed down with bangles.

PROSPERO:
Thou, my slave,
As thou report'st thyself, wast then her servant;

40.18 With Ariel's head appearing out of the water in the foreground – immediately behind him is the mirror-image of his adventures sixteen years before on his first night with Sycorax on the island. *Mirror-image*: Ariel sits on the sand on the moonlit beach . . . and looks around him.

40.19 *Mirror-image*: At a harsh, female cry from within the palanquin . . . and pushed and shoved by the retinue of dwarfs – Ariel is jerked to his feet and dragged – with a long chain – behind the palanquin as it is pulled and pushed up the beach.

40.20 *Mirror-image*: The mirror-bearers splash the mirror with bath-water and the reflection changes . . . to . . . a tent lit with candles . . . whose flapping walls are covered in scrawls, words and blood-smears. Lying on a couch, surrounded by horses . . . a naked Sycorax holds court – her body inexpertly covered in white chalk – her face masked with a black bag tied with laces – her head bald – with a greased and diseased body – very pregnant . . . her distended belly covered in tat-tooes and scratch-marks – her fingers and wrists bandaged.
She is surrounded by masked fauns. Ariel – tied with coloured ribbons – and held by fauns – is being forced to kiss a decayed head. He screams his resistance.

PROSPERO:
And, for thou wast a spirit too delicate
To act her earthy and abhorred commands,
Refusing her grand hests . . .

40.21 *Mirror-image*. Water-splashed – the reflec-tion changes to a moonlit night among pine trees . . . a screaming Ariel – held by fauns – is tied to a forked pine tree. The fauns – with mallets – drive wooden pegs – apparently – through his body into the pine-trunk – the dead-head he refused to kiss is tied around his neck.

PROSPERO:
. . . she did confine thee,
By help of her more potent ministers,
And in her most unmitigable rage,
Into a cloven pine;

40.22 *Mirror-image*: Time passes. Ariel's white body becomes indistinguishable from the pine-trunk – the death's-head has become a skin-covered skull . . . Ariel screams with wide-open mouth . . . a storm-wind rips across the tree – which is lit by flashes of lightning.

PROSPERO:
. . . within which rift
Imprisoned thou didst painfully remain
A dozen years;

40.23 *Mirror-image:* Time passes. It is raining hard – Ariel moans piteously from deep within the tree – his finger-ends, his mouth – still visible . . . the death's-head is now a skull without a lower jaw.

PROSPERO:
. . . within which space she died,
And left thee there; where thou didst vent thy groans
As fast as mill-wheels strike

40.24 *Mirror-image*: Water is splashed across the mirror and the image changes. A cave-room – a pit half below-ground – a floor of bones and stones and large shells. On soiled sheets – Sycorax – bent double like a hoop – is trying to give birth – she screams and yells . . . creatures surround her . . . ugly fauns and ancient nereids with hanging breasts. Prospero is trying to act as midwife . . . a spotted, fat baby – more like a piglet than a human child – is produced in a welter of blood and pus and maggots and the sound of buzzing flies . . .

PROSPERO:
Then was this island –
Save for the son that she did litter here,

A freckled whelp, hag-born – not honoured with
A human shape.

40.25 *Mirror-image*: Ariel, imprisoned in the pine tree – has vanished except for his crying, moaning mouth . . .

PROSPERO:
Thou best know'st
What torment I did find thee in: thy groans
Did make wolves howl, and penetrate the breasts
Of ever-angry bears. It was a torment
To lay upon the damned, which Sycorax
Could not again undo.

40.26 *Mirror-Image*: . . . Ariel in the pine tree is set free. With a loud, painful scream – pulling and stretching and the sound of ripping . . . Ariel emerges from the bark, moss and lichen . . . his body bloody. He stands in the light – moaning with pain . . . the blood running from around his neck, his armpits and groin . . . as we watch . . . the running blood disappears and his body – white in the light – is faintly marked with tree-rings . . . these too slowly vanish.

PROSPERO:
It was mine Art,
When I arrived and heard thee,
*   that made gape*
The pine, and let thee out.

40.27 Prospero's face – benign but admonishing.

PROSPERO:
If thou more murmur'st, I will
*   rend an oak,*
And peg thee in his knotty
*   entrails, till*
Thou hast howled away twelve
*   winters.*

40.28 Ariel bows . . . and rises from the water and frees himself from the water-meniscus . . . and then begins to jump

and dance – as on a springboard, turning and somersaulting in the air . . . his body gradually turning into the colours of the seas and oceans – emerald, turquoise, blue and green.

PROSPERO (playing Ariel):
Pardon, Master.
I will be correspondent to command,
And do my spriting gently.
(playing himself):
Do so; and after two days
I will discharge thee.
(playing Ariel):
That's my noble master!
What shall I do? Say what! What shall I do?
(playing himself):
Go, make thyself like a nymph o' the sea:
Be subject to
No sight but thine and mine; invisible
To every eyeball else.
Fine apparition! My quaint Ariel,
Hark in thine ear. (He whispers)

40.29 Ariel descends from his floating position and puts his ear to Prospero's mouth – his whole

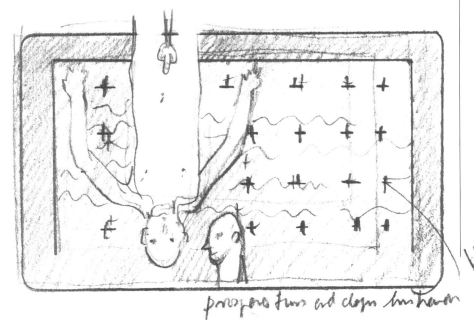

prospero turns and closes his hands

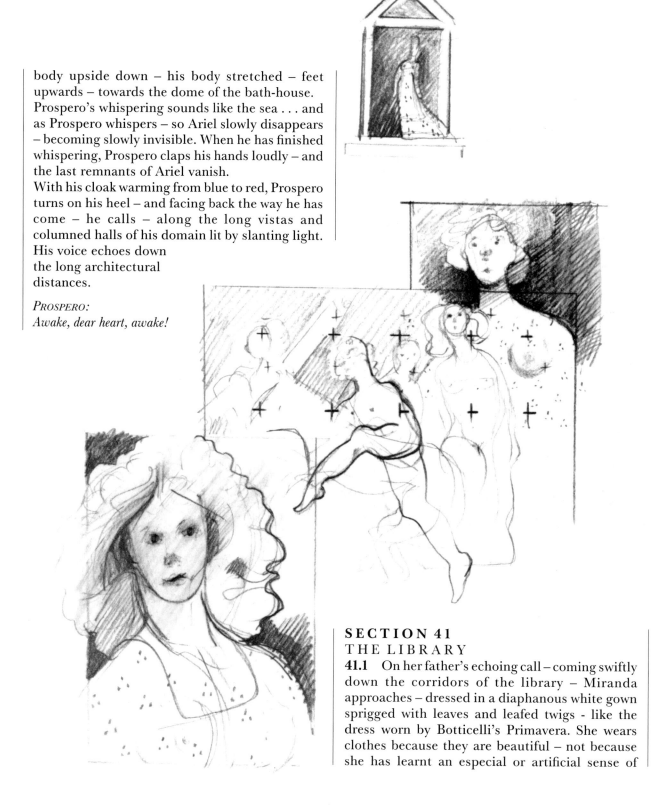

body upside down – his body stretched – feet upwards – towards the dome of the bath-house. Prospero's whispering sounds like the sea . . . and as Prospero whispers – so Ariel slowly disappears – becoming slowly invisible. When he has finished whispering, Prospero claps his hands loudly – and the last remnants of Ariel vanish.

With his cloak warming from blue to red, Prospero turns on his heel – and facing back the way he has come – he calls – along the long vistas and columned halls of his domain lit by slanting light. His voice echoes down the long architectural distances.

PROSPERO:
Awake, dear heart, awake!

SECTION 41
THE LIBRARY

41.1 On her father's echoing call – coming swiftly down the corridors of the library – Miranda approaches – dressed in a diaphanous white gown sprigged with leaves and leafed twigs - like the dress worn by Botticelli's Primavera. She wears clothes because they are beautiful – not because she has learnt an especial or artificial sense of

LOOKING FOR IMAGES OF MIRANDA,
THIS BOTTICELLI IMAGE OF SPRING COULD BE
A CLASSICAL DEITY NOT OUT OF PLACE
IN THE FOREST OF ARDEN.

modesty. Her breasts, her hips, her belly are seen through the moving folds. She is an innocent sent to destroy the fiercest prude.

She comes to a slow halt when the echoes of Prospero's call die away. She appears to be sleep-walking. She has stopped by Prospero's writing-desk – where the 'real' Prospero is glimpsed through curtains – writing by bright candlelight. The 'real' Prospero stops writing and looks up at his daughter, who doesn't see him.

41.2 Medium close-up of Prospero – pen poised – looking at his daughter. He stares at her.

PROSPERO:
Awake, dear heart, awake.

His own voice – as master-manipulator – awakens her from her somnambulism. Before she can fully respond – Prospero – almost without looking at what he is writing – writes 'Awake, dear heart' in his book ... at the same time – Prospero's off-screen voice calls out the same words and Miranda – hearing them, hurries towards the bath-house.

41.3 A wide shot of the library – where one of the library's mythological figures – a lithe young cen-taur – a combination of small pony and boy – for a moment runs alongside her – before he is pulled back by two dark nymphs who carry rolls of paper and quills.

SECTION 42
THE BATH-HOUSE
42.1 Miranda enters the bath-house and stands momentarily back-lit against the light – her body beneath the robe sharply contoured – her long hair blowing ... she momentarily searches in the warm darkness for her father ...

PROSPERO (playing Miranda, in a whisper):
The strangeness of your story put heaviness in me.

42.2 Prospero watches her ... as he stands by the pool – the water reflecting across his body.

PROSPERO:
Come on: we'll visit Caliban, my slave, who never yields us kind answer.

42.3 Miranda holds back – but Prospero takes her hand ... and she lets herself be led around the pool where their reflections light up in the water ... and on into the shadowy spaces of the rows of columns beyond.

SECTION 43
CALIBAN'S PIT

43.1 Prospero and Miranda approach Caliban's pit. It is a dank pool in a square pit – with sheer walls – like a hippopotamus-pool in a Victorian zoo. The water – of unknown depth – but seemingly bottomless – is brown – almost black – with vegetable matter floating in it – not water-weed – but uprooted grass or cabbage-leaves. An unwholesome place – the drab walls are stained with lime that has leached out of the rock, and algae that is fed with slow seepage through the walls. In the very centre of this square pit of unpleasantness – rising up out of the water – is a crumbling brick tower – covered in decaying concrete. Up the side of it runs a ladder of rusting iron hoops. This island tower has a lower ledge that is barely covered by the trembling murky water. There is evidence – by the ring-marks around the walls – that the water-level of the pit is never constant – but moves up and down. In a dry season, we may surmise – it falls very low. In a wet season, the water might rise to flood over the very top of the brick pillar. We can see the 'seasonal' cause – a circular ceramic pipe – large enough to house a pig – and much stained – empties effluent into the water; whilst we watch – it gurgles from deep within and a sludgy brown fluid disgorges into the murk – followed by a rush of brown liquid which diminishes to a trickle and then drips ... this source of distaste is like a tunnel to a distant privy used by incontinent giants.

On the top of the island-refuge are clumps of wretched grass and weed – fireweed, chickweed, groundsel, plantains, dandelions – weed that colonises bare, bleak and inhospitable places – that are much scuffed, stubbed and abused. The entire pit lies in a cold shadow. Gnats dance in a shaft of brown light.

Leaning against the tower at the water-line – is a mirror – it's been splashed with dirty water and is stained and cracked, but still serviceable.

43.2 Prospero peering into the deep pit shouts, his voice bellowing back at him from the echoic walls.

PROSPERO:
What ho! slave! Caliban!
Thou earth, thou, speak!
Thou poisonous slave, got by the devil himself
Upon thy wicked dam, come forth!

There is movement – the brown murk shivers – up from its depths – like Grendel moving from subterranean caves – moves an ambiguous creature – snorting like a hippopotamus with fat wet brown flanks . . . it rolls over – showing a dark-pink underbelly and pink nipples – it is certain that it has limbs – it is not a fish – yet it seems suited to water . . . it duck-dives – its buttocks shining in the dull light . . .

43.3   With occasional quick surfacings – leaving trails of bubbles and froth and swirls of cabbage-leaves – Caliban – still keeping his form and shape anonymous in the gloomy light and dark water – speaks.

Prospero (playing Caliban):
As wicked dew as e'er my mother brushed
With raven's feather from unwholesome fen,
Drop on you both!

43.4   *Mirror-image*: In Caliban's cracked mirror on the water-ledge of his tower . . . an image – at dawn, the naked, thin-legged, very pregnant, leather-hooded Sycorax wields – like a scythe across the tops of dark, sweating plants in a swamp – a decayed, black-feathered wing . . . or a whole bird – all bones and beak and feathers – a crow or rook or raven stiff with rigor mortis

43.5   *Mirror-image*: In Caliban's cracked mirror. Prospero and Miranda dressed identically as they are beside the pool . . . are shielding their faces against being violently spattered with blood-coloured, sticky fluid.

Prospero (playing Caliban):
A south-west blow on ye,
And blister you all o'er!

In Caliban's mirror . . . Prospero and Miranda – covered in the blood-coloured fluid – are violently showered with black feathers that stick to their torsoes and faces.

43.6   Prospero – with an anger which undoubtedly is part feigned – flings high his left hand . . . and Caliban's mirror shatters some more – but it still does not break completely. Prospero paces up and down the edge of the pool. Miranda hangs back.

43.7   In dark crevices in the pit walls – under the sluice-pipe and among the loose bricks of the island – it is possible to see half-glimpsed creatures of malign intent – scab-faced fauns, leprotic children.

Prospero:
For this, be sure, tonight thou shalt have cramps,
Side-stitches that shall pen thy breath up; urchins
Shall forth at vast of night that they may work,
All exercise on thee; thou shalt be pinched
As thick as honeycomb, each pinch more stinging
Than bees that made 'em.

43.8   *Mirror-image*: In Prospero's mirror – carried forward from the shadows by malfigured creatures – a naked, ambiguous body, in a wicker basket of green nettles – (without giving away too much identity – it is Caliban) – curled foetus-like and protecting its genitals – is pinched and poked by long-handled, metal pincers.

43.9   Caliban continues to elude full corporeal identity – though we realise now he has hands and feet. He continues to break the surface with swishing strokes and some splashing.

Prospero (playing Caliban):
This island's mine, by Sycorax my mother,
Which thou tak'st from me. When thou cam'st first,
Thou strok'dst me, and made much of me;

43.10   *Mirror-image*: In Caliban's cracked mirror . . . on a shining, moonlit beach – with the surf behind them – surrounded by piles of exotic shells and books – prominent among them the *Book of Travellers' Tales* . . . Prospero kneels with two infants – Miranda and Caliban – and points out the moon. The child Caliban is dark and swarthy with a large shock of black hair. It is Miranda who is wayward – splashing in the surf – throwing up back-lit water.

Prospero (playing Caliban):
. . . wouldst give me
Water with berries in't; and teach me how

To name the bigger light, and how the less,
That burn by day and night.

43.11   Ambiguous underwater shots of Caliban –
swimming and diving effortlessly in the murky
brown water – a top-lit soup of cabbage-leaves,
turnip-tops, peelings, rind, toads and bones.

PROSPERO (playing Caliban):
And then I loved thee,
And showed thee all the qualities o'the isle,
The fresh springs, brine-pits, barren place, and fertile.

43.12   Caliban surfaces in a very dark corner –
under the brick tower – his features dim in the
gloom.

PROSPERO (playing Caliban):
Cursed be I that did so! All the charms
Of Sycorax, toads, beetles, bats, light on you!
For I am the all the subjects that you have,

Which first was mine own king! And here you sty me
In this hard rock, whiles you do keep from me
The rest o'th'island.

43.13   Prospero – now peering into the murk – is
becoming genuinely irritated.

PROSPERO:
Thou most lying slave,
Whom stripes may move, not kindness! I have used thee,
Filth as thou art, with human care, and lodged thee
In mine own cell, till thou didst seek to violate
The honour of my child.

43.14   This is the signal for Caliban to fully reveal
himself. He surfaces with an explosive grunting
laugh and sits, straddled-legged, on the low part of
the pit's island-platform – showing with brazen ex-
hibitionism his mandrill-coloured genitals –
bright-blue scrotum, orange penis, pink groin and
vermillion anus.

Caliban is at last fully seen – a travesty of a mortal – somewhat like a young Silenus – he has small, gnarled and curled horns, and on close inspection he is seen to have a small and ridiculous tail – the small of his back is patterned with black markings like a mottled pig.

PROSPERO (playing Caliban):
Oh ho! Oh ho! Would't had been done!
Thou didst prevent me; I had peopled else
This isle with Calibans.

We can see that Caliban has been holding tightly on to a thick, heavy book – which he opens at a double page of black-and-white illustrations – it doesn't seem to have suffered from being submerged in the dirty water. It is a book belonging to Prospero which Caliban has stolen. It is *The Ninety-Two Conceits of the Minotaur.*

43.15 A close-up of the open, black-paged, double spread of Caliban's book – showing copulating devils. Caliban has reason to steal this book ... for being *The Ninety-Two Conceits of the Minotaur* it reflects on the experiences of the most celebrated progeny of bestiality ... the Minotaur ... with an impeccable classical mythology to explain its provenance ... Daedalus and Icarus, Theseus and Ariadne. Since Caliban – along with centaurs, mermaids, harpies, the sphinx (and

CHAINED TO A ROCK, MICHAEL CLARK AS A WATER-LOVING CALIBAN, IS IMPRISONED AT THE CONFLUENCE OF SIX SEWERS.

vampires and werewolves) – is the result of bestiality, he would be interested. The book – mocking Ovid's *Metamorphoses* – tells the story of ninety-two hybrids . . . it should have told 100 – but the puritanical Theseus had heard enough and slew the Minotaur before he could finish. When opened, the book exudes yellow steam and coats the fingers with black oil.

43.16   Prospero – now really angry – shouts down at the laughing Caliban who – with considerable agility – hoists himself up several rusty rungs of the ladder . . . and hangs there – smirking and playing with himself.

PROSPERO:
Abhorred slave,
Which any print of goodness wilt not take,
Being capable of all ill! I pitied thee,
Took pains to make thee speak, taught thee each hour
One thing or other.

43.17   *Mirror-image*: In Prospero's mirror: in his study, Prospero has sat Miranda and Caliban side by side on a bench and surrounded them with books.

PROSPERO:
When thou didst not, savage,
Know thine own meaning, but wouldst gabble like
A thing most brutish, I endowed thy purposes
With words that made them known.

43.18   *Mirror-image*: A close-up of another Prospero book – *The Book of Languages*. It is a large, thick book . . . old . . . with a multi-coloured cover that rainbow-hazes in the light. It opens in unorthodox fashion with a door in its front cover. Inside there is a collection of eight smaller books arranged like bottles in a medicine case. Behind these eight books are another eight books, and so on – the interior of the book does not seem to correspond to the capacity of the exterior. Opening the smaller books is to let loose many languages . . . words and sentences and paragraphs gather like black tadpoles or flocking starlings . . . accompanied by a great noise of babbling voices.

PROSPERO:
But thy vile race,
Though thou didst learn, had that in't which good natures
Could not abide to be with. Therefore wast thou
Deservedly confined into this rock,
Who hadst deserved more than a prison.

43.19   Caliban now climbs adroitly to the top of the brick island and raising himself up – replies with full impudence to Prospero.

PROSPERO (playing Caliban):
You taught me language; and my profit on't
Is, I know how to curse. The red plague rid you
For learning me your language!

Caliban hurls the book – *The Ninety-Two Conceits of the Minotaur* – at Prospero. Prospero deftly catches it . . . and smiles. He is amused, but he doesn't show it to Caliban – he feigns indignation, and standing tall – puts on a frightening display of wrath. His four dancing minions materialise from the columned shadows and begin to dance in an exact square about him – a dance of ingenuity and complexity with great discipline.

PROSPERO:
Hag-seed, hence!
Fetch us in fuel; and be quick, thou'rt best,
To answer other business. Shrug'st thou, malice?
If thou neglect'st or dost unwillingly
What I command, I'll rack thee with old cramps,
Fill all thy bones with aches, make thee roar,
That beasts shall tremble at thy din.

43.20   Caliban is intimidated. Prospero kicks a peg with his foot, and a simple plank bridge falls from the rock wall to make a bridge from the pit's edge to the brick-tower – Caliban crosses – making sure he is as far as possible away from Prospero.

PROSPERO (playing Caliban):
No, pray thee.
I must obey. His Art is of such power,
It would control my dam's god, Setebos,
And make a vassal of him.

Prospero – guiding Miranda leaves.

THE PRESENT

THE BASIC STRUCTURE, TIME, PLACE AND PROPOSED DIRECTION OF THE TALE ARE
NOW KNOWN TO US. THE ISLAND'S INDIGENOUS CHARACTERS HAVE ALL BEEN
INTRODUCED. PROSPERO'S PAST, PRESENT AND LIKELY FUTURE ACTION ARE
FIXED. THE FIRST THIRD OF THE NARRATIVE — MAINLY ABOUT THE PAST — HAS BEEN
TOLD . . . IN LIGHTING THAT HAS BEEN VERY VARIED BUT PREDOMINANTLY DARK
AND INTERIOR AND 'ARTIFICIAL'. WE NOW MOVE INTO THE SECOND THIRD WHICH
DEALS WITH PROSPERO'S MACHINATIONS FOR REVENGE . . . AND IS VERY MUCH IN
THE PRESENT TENSE. TO REFLECT THAT THE FILM MOVES NOTICEABLY INTO A CON-
TRAST MADE MOST MANIFEST BY LIGHT — THE BRIGHT LIGHT, THE NOON SUN, THE
WIDE PANORAMAS AND OPEN AIR THAT SUGGEST THE PRESENT TENSE.

SECTION 44
THE CORNFIELD

44.1   After the purple-and-grey darkness and implied malice of the Caliban pit . . . comes a brightly
contrasting sequence of golden sunlight where the
sun shines vertically down from a clear blue sky. It
is a vista seen from a wide balcony . . . a panorama
like a large Rubens landscape under a wide sky –
only the panorama is a curiously exotic one – an
island inhabited by the Italianate architectural
fantasies of an academic interested in antiquity
and classical mythology. It is a scene heralded by
magnificent and grand pastoral music – a golden
lyricism.

At the foreground centre of this panorama is a
large cornfield in perpetual harvest. Beyond the
cornfield on one side . . . on the horizon . . . is a
dark forest – the dark-green trees tossing in a
slight breeze . . . the crowns of the tall umbrella-
pines noisy with birds . . . parrots, crimson rooks,
long-tailed cockatoos. On the other side of the
cornfield is the beach and the sea . . . the cornfield
is on a strand . . . a wide finger of land stretching
out into the ocean.

Above the corn – in the middle-distance looking
towards the forest – rising up out of the golden
mass – is a gathering of pyramids. They are built of
different materials – grey stone, white marble, ter-
racotta-brick, yellow sandstone. Some pyramids
are edged and decorated in contrasting coloured
materials – some are missing their crowns, some
are ancient . . . all of them have a much more ex-
aggerated slope than would be expected of true
Egyptian pyramids – like pyramids that have been
enthusiastically built on the hearsay evidence of
travellers . . . that have been constructed by an
antiquarian like Prospero who obtained his knowledge from books, not first-hand observation. The
most dominant pyramid is of grey-and-white gra-
nite with a Latin inscription . . . though the inscription is impossible to read from this distance
. . . it is a pyramid very similar to the Pyramid of
Cestius in Rome . . . the regular blocks of its composition clearly visible in straight, horizontal,

THESE STEEPLY-RAKED PYRAMIDS,
ILLUSTRATING A TREATISE ON HIEROGLYPHS
BY KIRCHER, SUGGEST THE OBSERVATIONS OF AN
ACADEMIC RELYING ON TRAVELLERS' TALES.

parallel lines – eroded a little into a harmonious
whole.

Across the plain of the cornfield – in a diagonal
line stretching to the distant forest – are four tall
obelisks – each one a little different in size and

98

shape. The furthest two are surrounded by wooden scaffolding . . . looking closely, you can see that craftsmen are at work on the scaffolding, gilding the hieroglyphics.

Visible in the comparative foreground – marked out in the corn-stalks is a regular geometric maze . . . although difficult to appreciate from ground-level – it is very apparent from up on the balcony of Prospero's palace.

44.2 From under a decorated and heavily tasselled awning onto the wide balcony or parapet that commands this wide panorama . . . step Prospero and Miranda. Prospero is dressed in his cloak, which is coloured blue . . . and he wears a broad-brimmed hat with tassels – exactly like a cardinal's hat – but in blue to match his cloak. The

cloak itself is patina-ed with that water-silk texture that is synonymous with a cardinal's robe. To complete the connection – he also wears the long gloves (but in blue) of a cardinal. His magic wand is also somewhat like a crozier. From the intense top-light of a noon sun, the broad-brimmed hat throws his face into deep shadow – so that he appears to wear a dark mask – we cannot fathom his expression. Miranda is dressed as before – but she too wears a broad-brimmed hat that strongly shades her face. Both walk to the balustrade that surrounds the parapet and looks out over a deep incline of wide formal steps to the cornfield far below. Miranda is more intent on the book she

carries than on the view. It is a herbal . . . called *End-Plants*. It is one of Prospero's magic volumes, a thick block of a book with varnished wooden covers that have been – probably still are – inhabited by minute tunnelling insects. Miranda rests the book on the balustrade and opens it up. It is immediately surrounded by insects.

44.3 The pages of the book are stuffed with pressed plants and flowers and around it hover exotic butterflies and dragonflies and fluttering moths and bright beetles . . . and a cloud of golden pollen-dust.

44.4 A close-up of Prospero's face. Beneath the shadowing hat – we see him search the landscape – checking out who is in it.

44.5 We see what Prospero sees: the camera searches and finds three groups of people . . . like distant figures in a Breughel summer landscape.

FERDINAND MEETS MIRANDA IN A PERPETUALLY RIPENING CORNFIELD. THIS BREUGHEL IMAGE CONJURES THOSE WARM, DRY HARVESTING DAYS INFREQUENTLY AVAILABLE TO MORTALS.

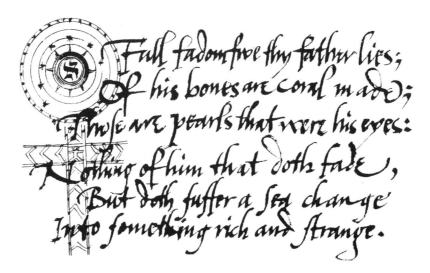

The farthest away – scarcely more than black-and-white dots – up against the fringes of the forest – are six men. The camera notes them and then pans across the landscape towards the beach where – separated one from another by sand dunes – are two small figures. Closest to hand – perhaps a quarter of a mile away – is a darkly-dressed young man in the cornfield – wandering – apparently lost – in the maze of deep alleyways through the corn which comes up to his shoulders.

44.6 Having seized on this last figure, the camera leaves the balcony and goes on a long travelling journey to take a closer look. The camera descends into the geometric maze mapped out in the corn-stalks . . . often losing sight of the darkly-dressed man . . . to see that the rows and rows of corn-stalks are made of gold – each stalk individually manufactured – like the legendary Aztec Eldorado golden cornfields – a stalk and leaves and a full head . . . stem after stem amassing into a golden sea . . . the camera eventually . . . moves slowly at the level of the full heads – down one of the alleys that make up the geometric maze. The lush lyrical music quietens . . . and backed by the sound of the distant sea and the singing of distant skylarks . . . and the breeze in the corn . . . and a distant bell . . . we hear singing . . . a child's voice . . . a soprano voice . . . the words are very clearly heard.

Full fathom five thy father lies:
Of his bones are coral made;
Those are pearls that were his eyes:
Nothing of him that doth fade,
But doth suffer a sea-change
Into something rich and strange.
Sea-nymphs hourly ring his knell.
Ding-dong.
Hark! Now I hear them – Ding-dong, bell.

As the camera continues to travel . . . it finds again – coming through a parallel pathway in the corn . . . the darkly-dressed young man . . . Ferdinand, the son of Alonso, the King of Naples. First we see his hat – a black, feathered extravagance – then his handsome head – with flowing black hair . . . and then his shoulders. The golden stalks reach as high as his chest – the cornheads regimented beneath the huge circularity of his white, laundered, extravagant ruff that sits around his neck like a giant cartwheel – making his head look decapitated on a glistening white plate.

He is lost. The bright sun shines vertically down – throwing his face into deep shadow under his broad-brimmed hat. After a pause . . . the voice of Prospero speaks for him.

PROSPERO (speaking a wondering, whispering, sad line for Ferdinand):
The ditty does remember my drowned father.

44.7 On the balcony . . . where Prospero and Miranda are standing . . . at the top of the broad flight of stone stairs that lead down into the cornfield . . . a decorated wreath of corn-stakes entwined with scarlet poppies and blue cornflowers falls at Prospero's feet . . . there is a swish of breeze – Prospero looks up.

44.8 A skein of poppies and corn-stalks trail in the sky before vanishing in whorls of corn-chaff and golden dust . . . it is the playful evidence of Ariel's passing.

44.9 Prospero smiles, and looking out over the cornfield – he touches Miranda's arm and points. She looks out over the brightly lit cornfield to see the distant figure. Prospero curiously and covertly watches Miranda as she looks.

44.10 He quietly voices her thoughts as she further shades her handsome face under the broad-brimmed hat . . . against the sunlight . . . to examine the distant figure. So intense is the top-light that her face in the shadow of her hand is – by contrast – very dark.

PROSPERO (playing Miranda):
What is't? A spirit?

44.11 Her curiosity is taken – she puts her book down on the stone parapet where Prospero has lain the wreath of corn-stalks and poppies. The book and the poppies and corn-stalks make a finely-composed *nature morte*.

44.12 Prospero – watching Miranda's face very closely – speaks for her.

PROSPERO (playing Miranda):
Lord, how it looks about! Believe me, sir,
It carries a brave form. But 't is a spirit.

This last line is delivered with some disappointment – as though Ferdinand is just another spirit of the island.
Miranda is almost on the point of turning away. She picks up her book.

44.13 Prospero takes her arm and begins to lead her down the broad stone steps that lead directly into the field of corn. She is still not entirely intrigued. She has taken a poppy from the corn-sheaf and placed it in her book as a marker.

PROSPERO:
No, wench; it eats and sleeps, and hath such senses
As we have, such. This gallant which thou seest
Was in the wrack; and, but he's something stained
With grief (that's beauty's canker), thou mightst call him
A goodly person.

44.14 In step, they walk down the stairs, disturbing some twenty white peacocks which have been sunning themselves.

PROSPERO:
He hath lost his fellows,
And strays about to find 'em.

The following is treated with serene slowness – a guileless emotional/sexual encounter – we watch the two protagonists fall in love – the central platform of Prospero's creation – the reason for all his other machinations . . . the lovers take on a state universally desired – reciprocal, uncomplicated, physical love. Supporting it is the Ceres bacchanal – a handsome coterie of mythological creatures from the paintings of Titian, Giorgione, Poussin . . . nymphs, fauns, maenads, putti, satyrs . . . with the conventionalised classical brown skin for the males, milk-white skin for the females.

44.15 Miranda walks forward. And looks at Ferdinand – who is oblivious of her presence. To the island's music – we watch her.

44.16 Her eyes are intrigued . . .

44.17 Her mouth begins to open . . .

44.18 . . . and a hand moves to her breast. We watch with fascination and with envy.

44.19 Prospero watches too . . .

PROSPERO (playing Miranda):
I might call him
A thing divine, for nothing natural
I ever saw so noble.

44.20 Ferdinand stands and looks about him – still oblivious (because of Ariel's magic) . . . of Miranda . . . and Prospero.

The Venetian painters Bellini, Giorgione and Titian might well have filled the scholarly head of a Milanese Duke with sensuous classical images like this Bacchus and Ariadne.

44.21 There is a chuckle from the corn ... the camera cranes up to see ... in an opening among the corn-stalks – a group of the island's mythological spirits ... they sit, kneel and lie like a lazy bacchanal in honour of Ceres. Naked figures wreathed in poppies and cornflowers and corn-wreaths – satyrs, fauns, nymphs, surround a full-breasted Ceres who is wreathed like a Queen of Harvest. Seated on Ceres' lap – is Ariel – with poppies and corn-stalks in his hair. He is consulting a book ... Ceres looks at the book over his shoulder ... pointing out something in the text. Ariel has become Cupid.

44.22 Close-up of the book. Bound in blue and gold – it is small and slim with red ribbons as bookmarkers. It is a book from Prospero's library – *The Book of Love*. We never see inside it – except later – in a mirror – and then only very briefly.

SECTION 45
PROSPERO'S STUDY

45.1 A contrast to the hot, bright sunlight – in the darker Rembrandtian light of Prospero's study ... with a gap in the curtains showing a long, sunlit perspective of the library – Prospero turns the pages of the small and modest, blue-and-gold *Book of Love*. He holds the book in such a position as to see a double-page spread of pages reflected in *The Book of Mirrors* ... where two idealised naked figures – a young man and young woman – are seen on one page ... and two hands clasped together are seen on the other (see Shot 89.13).

Prospero picks up his pen and writes in the *Tempest* book – whispering the words as he writes them.

PROSPERO:
As my soul prompts it.

SECTION 46
THE CORNFIELD

46.1 In the cornfield, Prospero smiles. Ariel leaves Ceres and walks triumphantly around Prospero.

PROSPERO:
Spirit, fine spirit! I'll free thee
Within two days for this.

The other cornfield figures join them to make a crowded mythological frieze across the screen. Strongly top-lit, their eyes are hidden in shadow ... a little golden corn-dust blows up to add to their mystery.

46.2 A 180-degree cut reveals – in contrast – the isolated figure of Ferdinand – still oblivious of their presence – listening to the singing – he continues to walk, turn, hesitate and stand – in his overdressed costume – a black-and-white, extravagant figure. Prospero ... speaks for Ferdinand.

PROSPERO (playing Ferdinand):
Most sure, the goddess
On whom these airs attend! Vouchsafe, my prayer
May know if you remain upon this island.

46.3   A medium close-up of Ceres – surrounded by her followers.

PROSPERO (playing Ferdinand):
And that you will some good instruction give,
How I may bear me here.

46.4   The isolated Ferdinand.

PROSPERO (playing Ferdinand):
My prime request,
Which I do last pronounce, is . . .

46.5   Ariel – creeping up behind Ferdinand – bounds into the air and places his hands over Ferdinand's eyes . . . and – with the same hands – manoeuvres Ferdinand – like a horse with a bridle – to face Miranda. Ariel then – with a flourish – takes his hands away and immediately leaps to Miranda and takes off her broad-brimmed hat – her long hair falls loose. Ariel's actions are swift . . . and even a little brusque. The lovers are rudely confronted with one another in an obvious gesture of matchmaking. There is a pause as the speechless Ferdinand takes in the image of Miranda.

46.6   Miranda – in the gown that scarcely hides her nakedness – is beautiful – top-lit by the high morning sun – which throws a deep shadow under her breasts and under her belly. Her hair blows. And she is flanked and backed by the horde of mythological figures, who are staring and smiling in expectation . . . one or two of them making the slightest of sexual gestures. The golden harvest dust blows stronger.

46.7   We watch the incomprehension on Ferdinand's face. Ariel – carrying *The Book of Love* – in which he quickly checks some fact – flies around behind him and takes off Ferdinand's broad-brimmed hat . . . and whispers in his left ear (courtesy of Prospero feeding him his lines):

PROSPERO (playing Ariel):
O, you wonder!

With dawning realisation – Ferdinand repeats Ariel's lines – we see him mouth them . . . though – again – it is Prospero speaking.

PROSPERO (playing Ferdinand):
O, you wonder!

Prospero plays his dialogue with very mixed feelings – with some irony he notes the expected effects of his matchmaking – of first love, of newly-aroused lust, of melancholy at his own long-lost love, and with some trepidation – for Prospero is in no doubt that his daughter – such an apparition of innocent sexuality – can make a powerful impression. As Miranda and Ferdinand stand facing one another over a short space of ground . . . he speaks their lines for them with the slightest affectionate mockery.

PROSPERO:
If you be maid, or no?

Ferdinand is still speechless – so Ariel – checking again in *The Book of Love* – flying behind him – repeats Prospero's words in his ear. Ferdinand – with passive obedience – repeats them . . . mouthing them – Prospero provides the sound.
46.8   Featuring Miranda with her mythological crowd. The dialogue progresses. Prospero – through Ariel who flies rapidly back and forth between the two young people . . . whispering in their ears – putting the words in both Ferdinand and Miranda's mouths.

PROSPERO (playing Miranda):
No wonder, sir;
But certainly a maid.

46.9   Featuring Ferdinand.

PROSPERO (playing Ferdinand):
My language! Heavens!
I am the best of them that speak this speech,
Were I but where 'tis spoken.

46.10   Featuring Miranda . . . joined by Prospero who, prompted by Ferdinand's arrogance, comes forward to stand beside his daughter.

PROSPERO:
How? The best?
What wert thou, if the King of Naples heard thee?

46.11   A wide shot to show the assembled company from the side. Miranda is in the centre – the fulcrum of the picture. Prospero and the mythological horde are on the left. Ferdinand – isolated – is on the right. They all stand in the shimmering golden cornfield – with the corn-stalks as high as their chests . . . backed by the prospect of the distant group of pyramids and the distant green forest of tall trees . . . Prospero . . . in his magic cloak – (dressed like a cardinal, but in blue) Miranda – naked under her diaphanous gown, and the black-and-white, overdressed Ferdinand.

PROSPERO (playing Ferdinand):
A single thing, as I am now, that wonders
To hear thee speak of Naples.

A pause – to fathom whether or not he is really witnessing these events.

He does hear me,
And that he does I weep.

A pause.

Myself am Naples,
Who with mine eyes, ne'er since at ebb, beheld
The King my father wracked.
PROSPERO:
The Duke of Milan
And his more braver daughter could control thee,
If now't were fit to do't.

Prospero speaks to Ariel, who is leaning against Miranda's legs. Ariel checks in *The Book of Love* – apprises some fact – and turns to deliberately tread on the hem of Miranda's gown pulling taut the cloth to further reveal Miranda's sensuous shape.

PROSPERO:
At the first sight
They have changed eyes. Delicate Ariel,
I'll set thee free for this.

46.12   Close-up of Ariel leaning against Miranda's legs – he blushes and then turns the colour of the corn – gold, brown, cream, white.
46.13   Medium shot. Ceres – assisted by a nymph

. . . comes forward and seizes Ariel by the waist and hoists him into the air . . . and swings around with him in a circle. After a complete spin – she lets go and he flies into the air. He drops *The Book of Love*. Ceres picks it up and gives it to Prospero.
46.14   In the bright, golden cornfield, the three protagonists – Prospero, Miranda and Ferdinand circle around one another.

PROSPERO (to Ferdinand):
I fear you have done yourself some wrong. A word.
(playing Miranda):
Why speaks my father so ungently? This
Is the third man that e'er I saw; the first
That e'er I sighed for. Pity move my father
To be inclined my way!
(playing Ferdinand):
O, if a virgin,
And your affection not gone forth, I'll make you
The Queen of Naples.
PROSPERO (aside):
They are both in either's powers. But this swift business
I must uneasy make, lest too light winning
Make the prize light.
(to Ferdinand):
I charge thee
That thou attend me. Thou dost here usurp
The name thou ow'st not: and hast put thyself
Upon this island as a spy, to win it
From me, the lord on't.
(playing Miranda):
There's nothing ill can dwell in such a temple.
If the ill spirit have so fair a house,
Good things will strive to dwell with 't.
PROSPERO:
Speak not you for him; he's a traitor.
(to Ferdinand).
I'll manacle thy neck and feet together;
Sea-water shalt thou drink; thy food shall be
The fresh-brook mussels, withered roots, and husks
Wherein the acorn cradled.
(playing Ferdinand):
I will resist such entertainment, till
Mine enemy has more power.

46.15 Just as Prospero has motivated Ferdinand with words – so now Ferdinand – prompted by a gesture from Prospero – raises his sword with a practised gesture – like one well-versed in fencing skills. Miranda is amazed, delighted . . . and alarmed.

PROSPERO (playing Miranda):
O, dear father,
Make not too rash a trial of him, for
He's gentle, and not fearful.
PROSPERO:
Put thy sword up, traitor;
Who mak'st a show but dar'st not strike, thy conscience
Is so possessed with guilt. Come from thy ward,
For I can here disarm thee with this stick,
And make thy weapon drop.
(playing Miranda):
Beseech you, father!
Sir, have pity. I'll be his surety.
PROSPERO:
Silence! One word more
Shall make me chide thee, if not hate thee. What!
An advocate for an impostor? Hush!
Thou think'st there is no more such shapes as he,
Having seen but him and Caliban. Foolish wench!
To the most of men this is a Caliban,
And they to him are angels.
(playing Miranda):
My affections
Are then most humble; I have no ambition
To see a goodlier man.
(playing Ferdinand):
My spirits, as in a dream, are all bound up.
My father's loss, the weakness which I feel,
The wrack of all my friends, nor this man's threats,
To whom I am subdued, are but light to me,
Might I but through my prison once a day
Behold this maid. All corners else o' the earth
Let liberty make use of; space enough
Have I in such a prison.
PROSPERO: (aside):
It works. Come on.
Thou hast done well, fine Ariel!

(playing Miranda):
Be of comfort.
My father's of a better nature, sir,
Than he appears by speech.
PROSPERO (to Ariel):
Thou shalt be as free
As mountain winds. But then exactly do
All points of my command.

Prospero – idly – consults *The Book of Love* he has in his hand . . . he then closes it – with his finger in a page – and clasps his hands casually behind his back and prepares to leave.

SECTION 47
PROSPERO'S STUDY

47.1 Prospero – in his study – speaks aloud – repeating himself.

PROSPERO:
Thou shalt be as free
As mountain winds. But then exactly do
All points of my command.

47.2 On his desk are two books – the herbal *End-Plants* we saw in Miranda's possession, and *A Bestiary of Past, Present and Future Animals*. Both books are open at double-spread illustrated texts showing apocryphal animals and plants in coloured line-drawings. The books are attended by objects associated with their content . . . the herbal is surrounded by orchids and bright berries . . . and the bestiary by a yellow-and-black lizard and a marmoset eating a small orange. In the centre of the desk, Prospero writes in his book the words . . . 'To the syllable.'
Ariel's shadow hovers above the white pages of the open book on Prospero's desk . . . and there is an echoic cry of the same words that moves around the spaces of the library.

47.3 All the candles in the library blow out . . . and the continuing cry of 'To the syllable' echoes out through the open door into the blinding white sunlight.

ACT II SCENE I
SECTION 48
THE CORNFIELD

48.1 From the balcony of Prospero's palace – a wide panoramic shot of the island landscape. We can see Prospero, Miranda and Ferdinand turning to walk in the direction of the balcony – but they are still way off in the corn.

The 'mythological' party is dispersing – scattering out down the various alleyways in the maze. The camera leaves them and, searching out towards the forest on the extreme left – picks up on an excited flock of birds wheeling and screeching above the treetops . . . something is disturbing them.

SECTION 49
THE FOREST

There follows a sequence that intercuts between the flora and fauna in the trees and their equivalents and near-equivalents in Prospero's books. The inference is that Prospero has populated the forests with his magic – using *End-Plants* and the *Bestiary* as his catalogues and templates.

49.1 With loud clapping/flapping wings – the birds fly in a bright blue/white sky where there is a daytime moon. They swoop lower where the camera follows to find the tree-canopy of the far forest we have seen beyond the cornfields.

In amongst the dense leaves and branches . . . there are parrots and monkeys, butterflies and flowers.

The camera descends slowly . . .

49.2 The pages of illustrations of *End-Plants* and the *Bestiary* turn to see many images (plus texts with key animal and plant nomenclature) of animals, fruits and plants – marmosets, hibiscus, chameleons, bats, climbing vine, crimson butterflies, snakes, pomegranates . . . the pages often littered with small leaves, berries, pollen-dust, maybe water-droplets – demonstrating that they are seen outside a library context.

49.3 As a bridge between drawing-and-painted-illustration and 'real' tree-canopy – some of the illustrations in the book themselves become still lifes – to match Prospero's imagination in inventing his story . . .

(1) A lizard on a pineapple on a book of pineapples.
(2) A butterfly settled on an orchid lying on a page of text.
(3) A monkey eating a cherry seated on an illustration of a monkey eating a cherry.
(4) A live tree-frog jumping from an illustration of plantain in a book.
(5) Stick insects walking over black-and-white engravings of plants.
(6) A turtle in a shallow, glass-bottomed dish of water resting on a book of fish.
(7) A snake crawling over a page of snakes.
(8) A parrot cracking nuts whilst standing on a page of illustrations of nuts.
(9) Snails crawling over images of snails.
(10) Ants running over a page of black text.
(and so on . . . with whatever small animals are available) . . . so that it is problematic to decide which is real forest and which is book illustration and which is still life.

49.4 In the 'real' forest, as the camera descends, the air is full of drifting seeds. The dense trees are now joined by standing marble columns – the same columns we are familiar with from Prospero's apartments – here the columns are covered in gold filigree vines – like the columns of Bernini's baldachino in St Peter's . . . the same gold vines are also twined around living trees.

We hear dialogue – Prospero speaking Gonzalo's lines.

PROSPERO (playing Gonzalo):
Beseech you, sir, be merry; you have cause,
So have we all, of joy; for our escape
Is much beyond our loss. Our hint of woe
Is common; every day, some sailor's wife,
The master of some merchant, and the merchant,
Have just our theme of woe; but for the miracle . . .

49.5 And then we discover the apparent source of the dialogue – six figures standing or lying in the grass and vegetation at the foot of the tall trunks

THIS YOUNG MAN PAINTED BY REMBRANDT
PROVIDES A MODEL FOR THE EFFETE
SHIPWRECKED NEAPOLITANS WHO HAD
STRONG DYNASTIC CONNECTIONS WITH THE
SPANISH NETHERLANDS.

and columns ... they are Alonso, Sebastian, Antonio, Gonzalo, Adrian, Francisco ... all elaborately and magnificently dressed – they make an approximate circle around Alonso. With their cartwheel ruffs, pendent jewelled earrings, feathered hats ... with jewels that flash and glitter, long legs tightly clad in white stockings, high buckled shoes on stilts, waxed and curled hair and beards, and a pronounced sexuality – breastplates showing muscled torsoes in the Roman style and prominent codpieces. Their artificiality mocks the extravagant fecundity and reality that surround them ... they are just this side of effete absurdity. They look dejected with the world-weariness of a bored court at a dull court-entertainment.

PROSPERO (playing Gonzalo):
... I mean our preservation, few in millions
Can speak like us: then wisely, good sir, weigh
Our sorrow with our comfort.
(playing Alonso):
Prithee, peace.
(playing Sebastian, aside, to Antonio):
He receives comfort like cold porridge.

49.6 As Prospero speaks each part – so the camera picks out each character in close-up.

PROSPERO (playing Adrian):
The air breathes upon us here most sweetly.
(playing Sebastian):
As if it had lungs, and rotten ones.
(playing Antonio):
Or as 'twere perfumed by a fen.
(playing Gonzalo):
Here is every thing advantageous to life.
(playing Antonio):
True; save means to live
(playing Gonzalo):
How lush and lusty the grass looks! how green!
(playing Antonio):
The ground, indeed, is tawny.
(playing Sebastian):
With an eye of green in't.
(playing Gonzalo):
But the rarity of it is, – which is indeed almost beyond credit ...
(playing Sebastian):
As many vouched rarities are.

SECTION 50
PROSPERO'S STUDY

50.1   In Prospero's study – lined up on his desk, are a collection of rarities – antiquities – jewelled rocks, decorated Venus-fruit, gilded skulls – exotic shells set in silver ... mixtures of the 'natural' and the 'man-embellished' – including the carapace of a green-and-yellow terrapin – these objects reflect the book illustrations we have just seen. Prospero – touching and handling these items – is seen to speak Gonzalo's lines.

PROSPERO (playing Gonzalo):
... that our garments, being, as they were, drenched
in the sea, hold, notwithstanding, their freshness
and glosses, being rather new-dyed than stained
with salt water.
Methinks our garments are now as fresh
as when we put them on first in Afric ...

50.2   From the curtains behind Prospero's writing-study, young women bring a full-length mirror that momentarily reflects Prospero and his study.
50.3   *Mirror-image*: Prospero's reflection disappears and is replaced by a picture of Prospero's imaginings ... and 'illustrates' Gonzalo's lines;

PROSPERO (playing Gonzalo):
... at the marriage of the King's fair daughter Claribel to

the King of Tunis.
(playing Sebastian):
'Twas a sweet marriage, and we prosper well in our
return.
(playing Adrian):
Tunis was never graced before with such a paragon to
their Queen.

In the mirror ... in a rich 'Arab-African' setting – tiled floor, ostrich fans, small fountains – Claribel, Alonso's fifteen-year-old daughter, the only white woman at a black African court, looks frightened and tearful. Arab, Negro and Egyptian courtiers, either naked with a sexuality that might shock a Christian European ... or else brightly dressed with much shining metal on their persons ... are present at a robing ceremony for Claribel's marriage to a fat, handsome, young black king with a large belly who reclines naked on a bed ... the

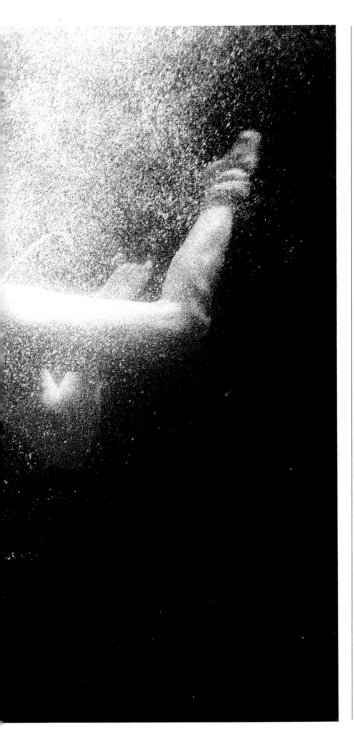

image is of a 1600s European fantasy of the Near Eastern Orient.

PROSPERO (playing Alonso):
Would I had never
Married my daughter there! for, coming thence,
My son is lost.

SECTION 51
THE FOREST

51.1   A wide shot of the forest, the figures dwarfed by the trees and columns.

PROSPERO (playing Alonso):
O thou, mine heir
Of Naples and of Milan, what strange fish
Hath made his meal on thee?

51.2   A two-shot of Alonso and Francisco, Prospero speaking Francisco's lines.

PROSPERO (playing Francisco):
Sir, he may live.

We see Francisco – he is making vigorous swimming strokes and miming the rescue of Ferdinand. The camera cranes down to look at the seated/reclining listening figure of Alonso.

PROSPERO (playing Francisco):
I saw him beat the surges under him,
And ride upon their backs; he trod the water,
Whose enmity he flung aside, and breasted
The surge most swoln that met him.

SECTION 52
PROSPERO'S STUDY

52.1   *Mirror-image*: In Prospero's study – Prospero sits writing at his desk. In the mirror supported by

FERDINAND, HURLED INTO DEEP WATER
FROM THE WRECK OF HIS FATHER'S
FLAGSHIP, IS RESCUED BY SEA-NEREIDS
SENT BY PROSPERO.

the nereids – rough green seas hurl and sweep. Prospero looks up . . . and we see . . . the naked Ferdinand endeavouring – with some success – to swim.

52.2 *Mirror-image*: Underwater shots of Ferdinand struggling to keep afloat.

PROSPERO (playing Francisco):
His bold head
'Bove the contentious waves he kept, and oared
Himself with his good arms in lusty stroke
To th'shore, that o'er his wave-worn basis bowed,
As stooping to relieve him: I not doubt
He came alive to land.

52.3 *Mirror-image*: Ferdinand is hurled on to a broad beach by a white wave – he lies spreadeagled on the sand – gulls wheeling over him.

SECTION 53
THE FOREST

53.1 Alonso in the forest buries his head in his arms.

PROSPERO: (playing Alonso):
No, no. He's gone.
(playing Sebastian):
Sir, you may thank yourself for this great loss,
That would not bless our Europe with your daughter,
But rather lose her to an African.

SECTION 54
PROSPERO'S STUDY

54.1 *Mirror-image*: In Prospero's mirror, held by weeping women and stern fauns, a scene at Alonso's court where a tear-stained Claribel, surrounded by wailing women, is – before Alonso – handed over to a group of Africans with exotic gifts.

PROSPERO (playing Sebastian):
You were kneeled to, and importuned otherwise
By all of us; and the fair soul herself

Weighed, between loathness and obedience, at
Which end o' the beam should bow.

54.2 *Mirror-image*: A close-up of Claribel's frightened and tear-stained face.

SECTION 55
THE FOREST

55.1 In the forest – a close-up of the wretched Alonso.

PROSPERO (playing Sebastian):
We have lost your son,
I fear, for ever: Milan and Naples have
More widows in them of this business' making
Than we bring men to comfort them:
The fault's your own.
(playing Alonso):
So is the dearest o' the loss.
(playing Gonzalo):
My lord Sebastian,
The truth you speak doth lack some gentleness,
And time to speak it in: you rub the sore,
When you should bring the plaster.
(playing Sebastian):
Very well.

SECTION 56
PROSPERO'S STUDY

56.1 Prospero in his study is looking at a book – *The Book of Utopias*. A book of ideal societies. With the front cover bound in gold leather and the back bound in black slate, with five hundred pages, six hundred and sixty-six indexed entries and a preface by Sir Thomas More. The first entry is a consensus description of Heaven and the last is a consensus description of Hell, for there are always some on earth whose ideal world is Hell.

56.2 Close-up of the red-and-black printed text. Most of the book is devoted to describing every known and every imagined social community – with illustrations that are taken straight from John White's American Indians.

Prospero looks up from his reading . . . to glance out of a small window . . . into the grounds of his library to see the natives we saw earlier – joined this time by more – like the American Indians of John White – dressed in feathers and woad – sitting and smoking and standing on a lawn among peacocks – the drawings in the book and the 'Indians' on the library-lawn are the same.

SECTION 57
THE FOREST

57.1   In the forest. A two-shot featuring Gonzalo and Antonio – they mock and gesticulate – a double-act.

PROSPERO (playing Gonzalo):

Had I plantation of this isle, my lord . . .
Antonio takes a bunch of nettle-like plants in a leather-gloved hand.

PROSPERO (playing Antonio):
He'd sow't with nettle-seed.

Sebastian picks and scatters a handful of seed from giant umbelliferi.

PROSPERO (playing Sebastian):
Or docks, or mallows.
(playing Gonzalo):
And were the King on't, what would I do?
(playing Sebastian):
'Scape being drunk, for want of wine.

SECTION 58
PROSPERO'S STUDY

58.1   With his *Book of Utopias* in front of him . . . poised in the act of writing . . . Prospero is looking out of his study window at the 'natives' of his island who are modelled on John White's American Indians . . . brown-skinned, naked, and wearing complex woad decorations, beads and a few long feathers . . . the men are smoking and talking and watching a group of four women

dancing. The original John White drawings drawn in The 1580s – one suspects – were ethnically accurate . . . but his European engraver has toned them down to suit European sensibilities – and made the Indians fit the classical tradition. At the same time as increasing their sexuality, the engraver has also made them more 'decent' to a European eye.

PROSPERO (playing Gonzalo):
I' the commonwealth I would by contraries
Execute all things: for no kind of traffic
Would I admit; no name of magistrate;
Letters should not be known; riches, poverty,
And use of service, none; contract, succession,
Bourn, bound of land, tilth, vineyard, none;
No use of metal, corn, or wine, or oil;
No occupation; all men idle, all;
And women too, but innocent and pure:
No sovereignty;
All things in common nature should produce
Without sweat or endeavour: treason, felony,
Sword, pike, knife, gun or need of any engine,
Would I not have; but nature should bring forth,
Of its own kind, all foison, all abundance,
To feed my innocent people.

SECTION 59
THE FOREST

59.1   Sebastian and Antonio mock Gonzalo.

PROSPERO (playing Sebastian):
No marrying 'mong his subjects?
(playing Antonio):
None, man, all idle; whores and knaves.
(playing Gonzalo):
I would with such perfection govern, sir,
T'excel the Golden Age.

The camera retreats whilst Sebastian and Antonio stand and extravagantly bow and scrape before the smiling Gonzalo . . .

PROSPERO (playing Sebastian):
'Save his Majesty!

PROSPERO (playing Antonio):
Long live Gonzalo!

. . . to find among the trees next to the camera . . . the Golden Age personified . . . John White Indians and classical, mythological figures camped on the grass – like a Titian feast of the gods.

59.2 Whilst Sebastian and Antonio bow and scrape . . . in mock servitude . . . Ariel steals up on the others, covering their eyes momentarily with his small hands . . . as they sit or crouch on the ground. He kisses each one on the face and they at once become drowsy.

PROSPERO (playing Gonzalo):
You are gentlemen of brave mettle; you would lift the moon out of her sphere, if she would continue in it five weeks without changing.
(playing Sebastian):
We would so, and then go a bat-fowling.
(playing Antonio):
Nay, good my lord, be not angry.
(playing Gonzalo):
No, I warant you; I will not adventure my discretion so weakly. Will you laugh me asleep, for I am very heavy?

59.3 With the ministrations of Ariel, all Alonso's company – save Sebastian and Antonio – begin to fall asleep – falling in abandoned positions of luxurious relaxation that recall a Titian bacchanal where the protagonists are drunk.

PROSPERO (playing Alonso):
What, all so soon asleep? I wish mine eyes
Would, with themselves, shut up my thoughts: I find
They are inclined to do so.

59.4 Ariel kisses Alonso, and he too falls asleep – falling back into Ariel's arms – who gently rests him back on a mound of flowered grass.

PROSPERO (playing Sebastian):
Please you, sir,
Do not omit the heavy offer of it:
It seldom visits sorrow; when it doth,
It is a comforter.

(playing Antonio):
We two, my lord,
Will guard your person while you take your rest,
And watch your safety.

SECTION 60
PROSPERO'S STUDY
60.1 Prospero, quickened by the imminent idea of conspiracy to murder, writes quickly in his open book . . . (for Sebastian): 'What a strange drowsiness possesses them!'
(and for Antonio): 'It is the quality o' the climate.'

SECTION 61
THE FOREST
61.1 Prospero speaking for them.

PROSPERO (playing Sebastian):
Why doth it not then our eyelids sink? I find not
Myself disposed to sleep.
(playing Antonio):
Nor I; my spirits are nimble.
Worthy Sebastian? Will you grant with me
That Ferdinand is drowned?
(playing Sebastian):
He's gone.
(playing Antonio):
Then tell me,
Who's the next heir of Naples?
(playing Sebastian):
Claribel.

SECTION 62
PROSPERO'S STUDY
62.1 *Mirror-image*: In Prospero's study, the mirror is held by childen and old women. In the mirror – a travelling shot that circles from an abused Claribel – weeping on her pillow – her backside bare and bleeding . . . in a room of blowing curtains and huge slaves – her husband, the King of Tunis, being washed and massaged and administered to by slaves.

PROSPERO (playing Antonio):
She that is Queen of Tunis; she that dwells
Ten leagues beyond man's life; she that from Naples
Can have no note, unless the sun were post –
The man i' the moon's too slow – till new-born chins
Be rough and razorable; she that from whom
We all were sea-swallowed, though some cast again,
And that by destiny, to perform an act
Whereof what's past is prologue; what to come,
In yours and my discharge.
(playing Sebastian):
'Tis true, my brother's daughter's Queen of Tunis;
So is she heir of Naples; 'Twixt which regions
There is some space.
(playing Antonio):
A space whose every cubit
Seems to cry out, 'How shall that Claribel
Measure us back to Naples? Keep in Tunis,
And let Sebastian wake.'

SECTION 63
THE FOREST
63.1 Shots of the sleeping courtiers.

PROSPERO (playing Antonio):
Say, this were death
That now hath seized them; why, they were no worse
Than now they are. There be that can rule Naples
As well as he that sleeps; what a sleep were this
For your advancement! Do you understand me?
(playing Sebastian):
I remember you did supplant your brother Prospero.
(playing Antonio):
And look how well my garments sit upon me;
Much feater than before: my brother's servants
Were then my fellows; now they are my men.
(playing Sebastian):
But, for your conscience . . .
(playing Antonio):
Ay, sir; where lies that? Twenty consciences,
That stand 'twixt me and Milan, candied be they,
And melt, ere they molest! Here lies your brother,
No better than the earth he lies upon,

If he were that which now he's like, that's dead;
Whom I, with this obedient steel, three inches of it,
Can lay to bed for ever; whiles you, doing thus,
To the perpetual wink for aye might put
This ancient morsel, this Sir Prudence, who
Should not upbraid our course. For all the rest,
They'll take suggestion as a cat laps milk;
They'll tell the clock to any business that
We say befits the hour.

Ariel, sitting by Gonzalo, prepares to wake him.

SECTION 64
PROSPERO'S STUDY
64.1 In Prospero's study – in close-up – Prospero writes quickly the words of a song that Ariel sings:

ARIEL:
While you here do snoring lie,
Open-eyed conspiracy
His time doth take.

SECTION 65
THE FOREST
65.1 On the forest floor.

PROSPERO (playing Sebastian):
Thy case, dear friend,
Shall be my precedent; as thou got'st Milan,

I'll come by Naples. Draw thy sword: one stroke
Shall free thee from the tribute which thou payest;
And I the King shall love thee.
(playing Antonio):
Draw together.

As Sebastian and Antonio draw their swords and
prepare to strike – Ariel sings – into Gonzalo's ear.

ARIEL:
If of life you keep a care,
Shake off slumber, and beware:
Awake! Awake!
PROSPERO (playing Gonzalo):
Now, good angels, preserve the King!

(The others wake)

What's the matter?
(playing Sebastian):
Whiles we stood here securing your repose,
Even now, we heard a hollow burst of bellowing
Like bulls, or rather lions: did't not wake you?
It struck mine ear most terribly.

As if in answer to this lie – there is indeed the
sound of animals bellowing … though what
animal it is is unidentifiable. Mingled with the
animal noise is the sound of distant thunder – for
there is a storm approaching.

65.2   There now begins a long travelling shot.
The camera begins to slowly move as the characters get up – they soon begin to follow it – fearfully
looking over their shoulders at the imaginary
beasts.

Ariel, flying overhead, ties the courtiers with ribbons which he tugs and pulls, encouraging them to
move faster and faster as if to keep pace with the
camera. The thunder is louder.

PROSPERO (playing Antonio):
O, 'twas a din to fright a monster's ear,
To make an earthquake! sure, it was the roar
Of a whole herd of lions.

The camera goes faster, the angle abruptly changes,
and the characters appear to pass through an
archway decorated with stone lions. A group of
mythological children scatter into the trees as the
characters rush forward.

PROSPERO (playing Alonso):
Heard you this, Gonzalo?
(playing Gonzalo):
Upon mine honour, sir, I heard a humming,
And that a strange one too, which did awake me:
I shaked you, sir, and cried: as mine eyes opened,
I saw their weapons draw: there was a noise,
That's verily. 'Tis best we stand upon our guard,
Or that we quit this place: let's draw our weapons.
(playing Alonso):
Lead off this ground; and let's make further search
For my poor son

PROSPERO (playing Gonzalo):
Heavens, keep him from these beasts!
For he is, sure, i' the island.

The camera now swings in behind the running figures and looks into the direction they are running – a long double parallel avenue of trees and columns that looks like a tunnel – beyond are the palaces and towers of Prospero's palace – for the moment Alonso and his followers are too pre-occupied to see them. Ariel flies and flutters overhead like a Raphael putto.

ACT II SCENE II
SECTION 66
PROSPERO'S STUDY

66.1   To exactly match the image of the flying Ariel as a Raphael putto – the moving camera follows Ariel in flight across a deep-green forest painted on a canvas curtain . . . Ariel – dropping his pink and scarlet ribbons – mixes into his own exact painted image – a painted image grown a little old and a little paint-distressed – we see that the canvas curtains (fringed and tasselled) hang on rings and a rail that encloses Prospero's cell. As the 'real' pink and scarlet ribbons – multiplying all the time – fall and twirl to the ground . . . a myth-ological group – two young nereids holding large conches and carrying swans . . . pull the curtains apart (the curtains divide the body of the painted Ariel in half) . . . to reveal Prospero sitting at his desk, writing.

The nereids gather up the ribbons which have now reproduced themselves a thousandfold and the camera follows them into Prospero's study . . . The nereids exit out the back of the study, now fes-tooned in the red ribbons . . . and the camera observes Prospero in his study with his books . . . turning over pages of animal history . . . pages of apes, hedgehogs, fish, eels, parrots and adders, fish and amphibians . . . and of creatures that are devil-insects, devil-sprites, scorpions and fanciful things that bite and scratch and sting and pinch.

66.2   A small green terrapin walks across the animal-images in an open book of shelled and carapaced creatures – some known, most unknown and apocryphal.

66.3   Prospero – half playfully and self-mock-ingly – in the manner of an orthodox wizard – chants a spell as he writes down the word 'Caliban' in his book.

PROSPERO:
All the infections that the sun sucks up
From bogs, fens, flats, on Prosper fall, and make him
By inch-meal a disease! His spirits hear me,
And yet I needs must curse.

A wind blows the pages of Prospero's books – and giant cloud-shadows pass over him.

The camera retreats and eight playful mytholog-ical creatures carrying snakes pull the curtains to-gether to hide Prospero. On the curtain this time is painted . . . (old and distressed) a view of a sea-shore with an empty beach of ribbed sandbars in the foreground, and the wide flat horizon of the sea right across the picture . . . under a grey and white sky. The curtains themselves blow a little in a cross-wind, and are irregularly lit and shadowed by large clouds.

Suddenly, with a rush of music . . . a wild wind blows up the painted curtain image – splitting it open along its centre . . . to reveal . . .

SECTION 67
THE BEACH

67.1   . . . an exactly matched view of the same . . . a long, wide beach of ribbed sand covered in just six inches of ebbing salt water. The wind that was blowing the curtains is blowing all manner of things before it – leaves, rags, flags, birds, insects, pages of books. The distant clouds are grey and noticeably moving . . . threatening a storm. Occa-sionally there are flashes of lightning and rumbles of thunder. The whole scene is irregularly lit and shadowed as thick clouds pass over the sun.

Caliban enters from the right frame and proceeds

walking to the left – the camera keeping pace with him. He is carrying a pale, barkless tree-trunk, washed white by the sea. He splashes through the shallow water. There are the sounds of insects – wasps, bees etc. – on the sound-track. Caliban swats them wildly.

PROSPERO (his voice changed to play Caliban):
But they'll nor pinch,
Fright me with urchin-shows, pitch me i' the mire,
Nor lead me, like a firebrand, in the dark
Out of my way, unless he bid 'em: but
For every trifle are they set upon me;
Sometime like apes, that mow and chatter at me,
And after, bite me; then like hedgehogs, which
Lie tumbling in my barefoot way, and mount
Their pricks at my footfall; sometime am I
All wound with adders, who with cloven tongues
Do hiss me into madness.

SECTION 68
PROSPERO'S STUDY
68.1 Prospero's study – close-up of the green-and-brown terrapin walking across the pages of Prospero's *Bestiary*.

SECTION 69
THE BEACH
69.1 Suddenly Caliban grabs a green-and-yellow rag blowing in the wind, falls flat with a splash, and tries to bury himself in the water-covered sand – his limbs stuck out, he looks like a large, grotesque, green-and-brown terrapin.

For a moment we watch – the camera static – and wonder why he has done this. The answer is revealed – he has become frightened by Trinculo, who falls into picture from the right.

PROSPERO (playing Trinculo):
Here's neither bush nor shrub, to bear off any weather at all. If it should thunder as it did before, I know not where to hide my head. What have we here? a man or a fish? A strange fish! Were I in England now, as once I was, and

had but this fish painted, not a holiday fool there but would give a piece of silver: there would this monster make a man; any strange beast there makes a man: when they will not give a doit to relieve a lame beggar, they will lay out ten to see a dead Indian. Legged like a man! and his fins like arms! Warm, o' my troth! I do now let loose my opinion, hold it no longer: this is no fish, but an islander, that hath lately suffered by a thunderbolt.

Trinculo throws himself under Caliban's ragged cover at a loud clap of thunder.

SECTION 70
PROSPERO'S STUDY
70.1 On Prospero's desk is the *Book of Travellers' Tales*, open at a page that shows an ambiguous monster with four legs. On the opposite page are illustrated Gonzalo's 'marvels' (Shot 77.3) – ' . . . mountaineers dew-lapped like bulls, whose throats had hanging at 'em wallets of flesh' and ' . . . men whose heads stood in their breasts'. The illustrations are vivid and animated.
Prospero looks up and stares ahead.

PROSPERO (playing Trinculo):
Misery acquaints a man with strange bedfellows.

SECTION 71
THE BEACH
71.1 It's now pouring with rain. Stephano comes splashing through the water.

PROSPERO (playing Stephano):
What's the matter? Have we devils here? I have not 'scaped drowning to be afeard now of your four legs;

Caliban groans.

SCHEMING A PARODY OF HIS OWN USURPATION, PROSPERO PLANS THE CONSPIRACY OF CALIBAN THROUGH THE BOOK OF TRAVELLERS' TALES.

PROSPERO (playing Stephano):
This is some monster of the isle with four legs, who hath got, as I take it, an ague. If I can recover him, and keep him tame, and get to Naples with him, he's a present for any emperor that ever trod on neat's-leather.

Caliban groans.

He's in his fit now, and does not talk after the wisest. He shall taste of my bottle: if he have never drunk wine afore, it will go near to remove his fit. Come on your ways; open your mouth; here is that which will give language to you, cat: open your mouth; this will shake your shaking, I can tell you, and that soundly: you cannot tell who's your friend.
(playing Trinculo):
I should know that voice: it should be – but he is drowned; and these are devils: O, defend me!
(playing Stephano):
Four legs and two voices! A most delicate monster! His forward voice, now, is to speak well of his friend; his backward voice is to utter foul speeches and to detract. If all the wine in my bottle will recover him, I will help his ague.
(playing Trinculo):
Stephano! If thou be'st Stephano, touch me, and speak to me; for I am Trinculo.
(playing Stephano):
If thou be'st Trinculo, come forth: I'll pull thee by the lesser legs: if any be Trinculo's legs, these are they. Thou art very Trinculo indeed! How camest thou to be the siege of this moon-calf? Can he vent Trinculos?
(playing Trinculo):
I took him to be killed with a thunder-stroke. But art thou not drowned, Stephano? I hope, now, thou art not drowned. Is the storm over-blown? I hid me under the dead moon-calf's gaberdine for fear of the storm.
(playing Caliban, aside):
These be fine things, and if they be not sprites. That's a brave god, and bears celestial liquor: I will kneel to him. I'll swear, upon that bottle, to be thy true subject; for the liquor is not earthly.
(playing Stephano):
How now, moon-calf! How does thine ague?
(playing Caliban):
Hast thou not dropped from heaven?

(playing Stephano):
Out o' the moon, I do assure thee: I was the man i' the moon when time was.
(playing Caliban):
I have seen thee in her, and I do adore thee: My mistress showed me thee, and thy dog, and thy bush. I'll show thee every fertile inch o' the island;· And I will kiss thy foot: I prithee, be my god. I'll show thee the best springs; I'll pluck thee berries; I'll fish for thee, and get thee wood enough. A plague upon the tyrant that I serve! I'll bear him no more sticks, but follow thee, Thou wondrous man.
(playing Trinculo):
A most ridiculous monster, to make a wonder of a poor drunkard!
(playing Caliban):
I prithee, let me bring thee where crabs grow; And I with my long nails will dig thee pig-nuts; Show thee a jay's nest, and instruct thee how To snare the nimble marmoset; I'll bring thee To clustering filberts, and sometimes I'll get thee Young scamels from the rock. Wilt thou go with me?
(playing Stephano):
I prithee now, lead the way, without any more talking. Trinculo, the King and all our company else being drowned, we will inherit here.
(playing Caliban):
No more dams I'll make for fish; Nor fetch in firing At requiring; Nor scrape trencher, nor wash dish: 'Ban, 'Ban, Cacaliban Has a new master – get a new man.

ACT III SCENE I
SECTION 72
THE WOODYARD
72.1 A virtuoso, bravura shot that lasts for several minutes. The action takes place in two connecting courtyards which are used for the exercise of horses . . . and also – as now – temporarily used to store wood.

120

The shot starts with the camera viewing a high, brightly sunlit, unaccented, very solid, rusticated, cream stone wall that stretches parallel to the picture-plane from left to right and up to the very top of the frame. There is a grey cobbled yard at the front – a shallow stage. In the symmetrical centre of the high wall is a narrow, rounded arch which leads through a dark tunnel to another cobbled yard which we can presume is identical to the one we are standing in. In the far wall of this second cobbled yard is another arch leading to a third courtyard . . . and so it goes on to a vanishing point. The architecture – severely classical – is like a perfect exercise in perspective.

Flush to the wall in the near courtyard . . . and piled up high with precise regularity on the left-hand side of the tunnel . . . are thousands of black-painted logs – their sawn ends facing us. On the right-hand side of the tunnel, a second precisely regular pile is not nearly so high . . . and the sawn logs – of identical size and shape to the others – are painted white. Dark-green ladders are leant symmetrically against each pile of logs. A colour-scheme of cream and grey, black and white, with touches of dark green . . . all under a hot sun that shines straight down from a clear blue sky.

Ferdinand has been given an absurd task, a deliberately pointless punishment . . . to take the white logs into the far courtyard and bring the black logs into the near courtyard. An exercise to lower morale . . . like the military fatigue of painting coal white to discipline troops.

Ferdinand . . . stripped to his underclothes, which show the beginnings of tearing . . . and with a white canvas flour-sack draped across his shoulders to protect his skin . . . is laboriously carrying the logs from one courtyard to another. His body is very white and not made for manual work. It is dirty, scratched and puffy with bruising. There are long chains attached to his ankles which are tethered to a dark-green wooden mounting-post in the centre of the far courtyard. The tunnel is some twenty yards in length and in deep shadow – contrasting with the brightly-lit courtyards.

Because it is a horse-exercise yard . . . every now and again . . . fine white horses, saddleless and bridleless, trot, walk and canter in the courtyards – causing a dangerous hazard which Ferdinand has to avoid. Sometimes a group of horses gallops past the end of the tunnel – making the tunnel ring with the echoic clattering of their hooves . . . the horses are always riderless and unaccompanied.

The camera – with exact regularity – follows Ferdinand in and out of the tunnel . . . going with him when he retreats into the tunnel, retreating when he approaches the near courtyard . . . watching him climb the ladders, deposit the logs . . . and then return. The regularity of his occupation – methodically followed – is only broken by the random activities of the fine horses . . . an image of enslavement and liberty.

PROSPERO (playing Ferdinand):
There be some sports are painful, and their labour
Delight in them sets off: some kinds of baseness
Are nobly undergone; and most poor matters
Point to rich ends. This my mean task
Would be as heavy to me as odious, but
The mistress which I serve quickens what's dead,
And makes my labours pleasures.

Framed in sunlight, Miranda appears at the other end of the tunnel as Ferdinand walks towards her. Ferdinand does not stop his log-carrying . . . and Miranda is obliged to walk with him. The camera continues to follow them.

PROSPERO (playing Miranda):
Work not so hard: I would the lightning had
Burnt up those logs that you are enjoined to pile!
Pray, set it down, and rest you: when this burns,
'Twill weep for having wearied you. My father
Is hard at study; pray, now, rest yourself:
He's safe for these three hours.
(playing Ferdinand):
O most dear mistress,
The sun will set before I shall discharge
What I must strive to do.
(playing Miranda):
If you'll sit down,

I'll bear your logs the while: pray, give me that;
I'll carry it to the pile.
(playing Ferdinand):
No, precious creature;
I had rather crack my sinews, break my back,
Than you should such dishonour undergo,
While I sit lazy by.
(playing Miranda):
It would become me
As well as it does you: and I should do it
With much more ease; for my good will is to it,
And yours it is against.
You look wearily.
(playing Ferdinand):
No, noble mistress: 'tis fresh morning with me
When you are by at night. I do beseech you –
Chiefly that I might set it in my prayers –
What is your name?
(playing Miranda):
Miranda: – O my father,
I have broke your hest to say so!
(playing Ferdinand):
Admired Miranda!
Indeed the top of admiration! Worth
What's dearest to the world! Full many a lady
I have eyed with best regard, and many a time
The harmony of their tongues hath into bondage
Brought my too diligent ear: for several virtues
Have I liked several women; never any
With so full soul, but some defect in her
Did quarrel with the noblest grace she owed,
And put it to the foil: but you, O you,
So perfect and so peerless, are created
Of every creature's best!
(playing Miranda):
I do not know
One of my sex; no woman's face remember,
Save, from my glass, mine own; nor have I seen
More that I may call men than you, good friend,
And my dear father: how features are abroad,
I am skilless of; but, by my modesty,
The jewel in my dower, I would not wish
Any companion in the world but you;
Nor can imagination form a shape,

Besides yourself, to like of. But I prattle
Something too wildly, and my father's precepts
I therein do forget.
(playing Ferdinand):
I am, in my condition,
A Prince, Miranda; I do think, a King –
I would not so! – and would no more endure
This wooden slavery, than to suffer
The flesh-fly blow my mouth. Hear my soul speak:
The very instant that I saw you, did
My heart fly to your service; there resides,
To make me slave to it; and for your sake
Am I this patient log-man.

Finally, in the near courtyard . . . Ferdinand stops . . . and the lovers stand side by side – silently lost in mutual contemplation . . . whilst twenty fine white horses – with great curiosity – gather round them . . . tossing their manes, clattering their hooves in the echoic sunlit courtyard.

SECTION 73
PROSPERO'S STUDY

73.1 On Prospero's desk is a book – *The Book of Universal Cosmography* – which is full of exquisite diagrams of great complexity, demonstrating attempts to codify all universal phenomena in one system. They are like the drawings associated with Robert Fludd – complex, disciplined geometrical figures, concentric circles, lists arranged in spirals, catalogues arranged on a simplified body of man, the solar system – a mixture of the metaphorical and the scientific. The book is open at a great diagram showing the Union of Man and Woman – Adam and Eve . . . in a structured universe where all things have their allotted place (including horses) . . . and have an obligation to be fruitful.

73.2 Prospero is seated at his desk – which we now see is also carrying images of antiquity – marble busts, Roman inscriptions – tablets, fragments of tombs, architectural details. Prospero contemplates the diagrams in the book.

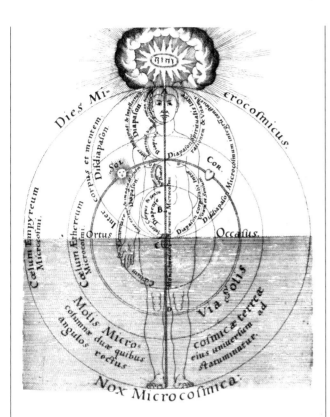

ROBERT FLUDD, TRYING TO CONNECT
ANGELS TO STONES, LEAD TO GOLD AND
MANKIND TO EVERYTHING, MANUFACTURED
METAPHYSICAL GRAPHICS TO STIMULATE
BELIEF IN A SINGLE UNIVERSAL ORDER.

PROSPERO:
Fair encounter
Of two most rare affections! Heavens rain grace
On that which breeds between them!

73.3 A close-up of the Adam and Eve figures in
the book, which reproduce the pose and composition of Ferdinand and Miranda in the next shot.

SECTION 74
THE WOODYARD
74.1 In the woodyard – as the camera circles . . .

reproducing the concentric circularity of the cosmographical drawings in Prospero's magic book
. . . the lovers continue to talk . . . surrounded by
the horses. Prospero – with great feeling – remembering his own past memories of love and erot-
icism – speaks for the lovers.

PROSPERO (playing Miranda):
Do you love me?
(playing Ferdinand):
O heaven, O earth, bear witness to this sound,
And crown what I profess with kind event,
If I speak true! If hollowly, invert
What best is boded me to mischief! I,
Beyond all limit of what else i' the world,
Do love, prize, honour you.
(playing Miranda):
I am a fool
To weep at what I am glad of.
At mine unworthiness, that dare not offer
What I desire to give; and much less take
What I shall die to want. But this is trifling;
And all the more it seeks to hide itself,
The bigger bulk it shows. Hence, bashful cunning!
And prompt me, plain and holy innocence!
I am your wife, if you will marry me;
If not, I'll die your maid: to be your fellow
You may deny me; but I'll be your servant,
Whether you will or no.
(playing Ferdinand):
My mistress, dearest;
And I thus humble ever.
(playing Miranda):
My husband, then?
(playing Ferdinand):
Ay, with a heart as willing
As bondage e'er of freedom: here's my hand.

74.2 A close-up of their joined hands which
Miranda draws towards her to hold between her
breasts, which are clearly seen through her dress.
Whilst still holding her left hand in his right, Ferdinand's left hand moves to hold her left breast,
whilst her right hand moves to hold her right
breast. It is an image of eroticism . . . but entirely

relevant to Prospero's book – a cosmographical emblem of unity, eroticism and fecundity.

SECTION 75
PROSPERO'S STUDY

75.1 A close-up in the *The Book of Universal Cosmography* . . . which reproduces in a line-engraving the image of the lovers' hands which we have just seen. The camera tracks down the desk, to see the following words written on the page – with the ink still drying.

PROSPERO (voice-over):
So glad of this as they I cannot be,
Who are surprised withal . . .

75.2 A medium shot. Prospero is at his desk – wrapped in his magic (dark blue) cloak – with the open *Book of Universal Cosmography* before him – set on top of the book where he is writing *The Tempest*. He has his pen in his right hand – just lifted from the page where he has written the above words. Golden sunlight shines on him. His four accompanying dancing spirits dance silently – almost on the spot – at the four corners of his desk . . . like brown and ochre shadows in the golden dust among the shelves and books of his library. He speaks aloud.

PROSPERO:
. . . but my rejoicing
At nothing can be more.

As well as having his scattered books around him, their loose pages flapping in a draught, he is surrounded by his antique collection – small marble obelisks, fragments of antique sculpture, stone heads, small tablet inscriptions . . . the collection of a dilettante antiquarian of 1611. In the centre of this collection is what looks like a solid piece of white marble veined in blue. Resting on it is a small, red, marble obelisk. He picks the red obelisk up in his left hand and – with his right hand – opens the white, blue-veined block of marble. It is a book.

75.3 Close-up. It is a book from his library – *Love of Ruins*. An antiquarian's handbook. A checklist of the ancient world for the Renaissance humanist interested in antiquity. Full of maps and plans and diagrams of the archaeological sites of the world . . . temples, castles, towns and ports, graveyards and ancient roads. Measurements and statistics of a hundred thousand statues of Hermes, Venus and Hercules, descriptions of every discovered obelisk and pedestal of the Mediterranean . . . street-directions in Thebes, Ostia and Atlantis . . . a directory of the possessions of Sejanus, the tablets of Heraclitus, the signatures of Pythagoras. An indispensable volume for the melancholic historian who knows that nothing endures. Its pages flick over rapidly – presenting a kaleidoscope of archaeological history which presages the next scene – where these objects – through Prospero's imagination – are made 'real'.

ACT III SCENE II
SECTION 76
THE 'ANTIQUARIAN' BEACH

76.1 A bravura, virtuoso travelling shot of several minutes. A section of foreshore with echoic music blowing on the wind. (Women's voices) whisperings very close, and miscellaneous dronings like giant insects or da Vinci flying-machines and an insistent rhythmic beat. The camera is already tracking on the empty beach – wind-blown objects pass by in a slow rolling motion against clouds – antique pages, manuscripts, sections of written scrolls . . . the wind is blowing in every direction. We see the origin of the ripped pages. The naked Caliban – with water glistening on his skin . . . wearing a huge canvas bag around his shoulder (it is stuffed with books) he is ripping out pages and tossing them into the wind.
Materialising against the white clouds of the sky is Ariel – he is in the very centre of the screen – flying, hovering, fluttering, swooping, rolling over, somersaulting . . . he flies in a tangle of bright red ribbons.

Coming from the right – suddenly dropping into the edge of the picture – is the long-haired Trinculo . . . he carries several giant exotic shells. His clothes blow and drag behind him like a white skin – attached to his wrists, his shoulders, his ankles, his collar . . . Vesalius-like.

After an interval – in the same way – the long-haired Stephano enters – naked save for his huge, grubby white, wide-brimmed hat that keeps blowing up at the front and the back like a grotesque Napoleonic hat . . . a huge, grubby, white cart-wheel ruff which somehow remains stiff and starched . . . and a grubby white codpiece secured with strings around his backside. His body is very white. All three creatures have been in the water. As the camera tracks at a steady pace – there are objects on the beach – buried columns – lying for centuries in the sand – their tops protruding – with evidence of much beneath the surface – the head of a statue, an obelisk . . . the evidence of a buried kingdom, a vast cemetery, a huge columbarium, an antiquarian's paradise.

PROSPERO (playing Trinculo):
Servant-monster! The folly of this island! They say there's but five upon this isle: we are three of them; if th' other two be brained like us, the state totters.

Larger objects now interrupt our view of the trio – stone statues still half buried . . . urns, busts, reliefs, tombs. Caliban walks adroitly around them. Ariel occasionally sits or squats on a stone head or astride a stone Pegasus – we are possibly in the graveyard – the memorial yard – of all classical mythology . . . all evidence of Prospero's cultural baggage. Caliban waves his hand at the objects of a far-off, foreign, unknown (to him) civilisation.

PROSPERO (playing Caliban):
As I told thee before, I am subject to a tyrant, a sorcerer, that by his cunning hath cheated me of the island.

Antique scrolls, papers, fly up into his face – he brushes them away irritably . . . the air is now full of the stuff – impossibly more than he can have ripped from his stolen books.

PROSPERO (playing Caliban):
*I say, by sorcery he got this isle;
From me he got it.*

Ariel – rolling out bright red ribbons – casually ensnares each of the trio as they walk and stumble along . . . winding the ribbons around their necks – he guides and pulls them along against the wind and the flying antique papers.

PROSPERO (playing Caliban):
*If thy greatness will
Revenge it on him, – for I know thou dar'st –
Thou shalt be lord of it, and I'll serve thee.*
(playing Stephano):
How now shall this be compassed? Canst thou bring me to the party?
(playing Caliban):
*Yea, yea, my lord: I'll yield him thee asleep,
Where thou mayst knock a nail into his head.*

They pass a group of statues – half buried in the sand . . . they turn out not to be statues but smoke-carbon-black-covered fauns. They hold spotted mirrors in ornate moulded frames.
Mirror-image: In the first mirror is a fleeting image of a naked, blindfolded, bound and gagged Prospero – wearing a tight-fitting doge's under-cap – hair askew – surrounded by piles of torn and ripped antique papers . . . with black billowing smoke in the background
Mirror-image: . . . In the second mirror is a close-up of the same – showing Prospero has a large nail driven into his head – up his nose.

PROSPERO (playing Caliban):
*'Tis a custom with him
I' the afternoon to sleep: there thou mayst brain him,
Having first seized his books; or with a log
Batter his skull, or paunch him with a stake,
Or cut his wezand with thy knife.*

As the camera continues to track along – more mirrors – held by dark fauns spirited out of the fallen statuary sometimes now tower over the trio.

We see reflected in the spotted mirrors –
(1) The image of Prospero asleep in his study . . .
(2) And then the mirror cracks and we see the top-pled Prospero of Caliban's wishful thinking – seen from different angles –
(3) . . . Bloodied in his studio – his antique frag-ments in violent disarray . . . an image with his brain smashed in, his naked stomach pierced by a large stake, his throat horribly cut.

PROSPERO (playing Caliban):
Remember
First to possess his books; for without them
He's but a sot, as I am, nor hath not
One spirit to command: they all do hate him
As rootedly as I.

The mirror-bearers cavort and stick out their tongues at the images in their mirrors – they run alongside the trio – the mirrors depicting the hor-rors they will all do to the fallen Prospero. Caliban flings more ripped pages into the air – and in great surprise – he is immediately showered with thou-sands of pages – mocking his efforts.

PROSPERO (playing Caliban):
Burn but his books.

In the faun-held mirrors, a brand is put to Pros-pero's books, which immdiately burst into flame – the whirling, twisting, burnt paper fragments blacken the mirrors . . . and contrast with the un-burnt whirling white pages that swirl about on the 'antiquarian' beach.
Struck by a thought, Caliban pulls up short – the camera does not stop tracking, and Caliban is swiftly left behind out of the frame on the left. Trinculo and Stephano continue.

PROSPERO (playing Caliban, voice-off):
And that most deeply to consider is
The beauty of his daughter; he himself
Calls her a nonpareil: I never saw a woman,
But only Sycorax my dam, and she;
But she as far surpasseth Sycorax
As great'st does least.

The whirling winds quicken.
Caliban catches up and leads the trio again – this time faster still – now among a veritable jungle of statues and tombs, cenotaphs and stone bric-à-brac from the classical world . . . that begins to dwarf them.

PROSPERO (playing Stephano):
Is it so brave a lass?
(playing Caliban):
Ay, lord; she will become thy bed, I warrant,
And bring thee forth brave brood.

The passing mirrors fleetingly depict the rape of Miranda in a palace of books . . . by the clumsy Ste-phano, who is all buttocks and belly . . . with a sweating red face.

PROSPERO (playing Stephano):
Monster, I will kill this man: his daughter and I will be
King and Queen – save our graces! – and Trinculo and
thyself shall be viceroys. Dost thou like the plot, Trinculo?
(playing Trinculo):
Excellent.

The lugubrious Trinculo struggles with his large hat and ruff in the wind. The mirrors – held by more and more dark spirits – depict four gaudy thrones in a row – we pass them severally – sitting on them are:
(1) A pale and sexually dishevelled Miranda with a tinsel crown.
(2) Then an overdressed, rubicund Stephano.
(3) Then a snotty-looking Trinculo – still in his giant ruff and codpiece.
(4) Finally Caliban – overdressed and absurd.
Suddenly there is a crash of music and the loud sound of Prospero's magic – the droning whine of great mechanical machines that always accompa-nies it – and the tracking camera – from having travelled faster and faster – suddenly stops dead – so suddenly – there is a feeling of vertigo.
Trinculo and Stephano are deeply frightened – they put their hands to their ears – they stoop and bend and cower – sticking their backsides towards the camera – they fear violent assault. The trio

have stopped among giant, Titanesque gods – huge muscular statues blowing conches – they could well be flesh, not stone . . . for there is the slightest suggestion of the wind blowing their long hair and beards – like Michelangelo sibyls. Ariel sits small and blithely cross-legged on a column in the centre of the picture – holding a tabor and pipe in either hand – holding them up as if to show he is not playing them, but there is a mighty orchestra at his command.

In a wide symmetrical picture, Caliban – realising the fright of his guests – swaggers a little and – deeply and genuinely appreciative of the music and its power – leans back against a giant red obelisk lying on its side – running away in perspective – it is a giant replica of the marble obelisk held in Prospero's hand when we last saw him in his study. Directly and symmetrically above Caliban – sits the grinning Ariel – together they represent the powers of the island – Ariel white and covered in back-lit golden light – smiling like a Sphinx of infinite power; Caliban – dark, brooding and evil – his eyes glinting in the shadows.

PROSPERO (playing Caliban):
Be not afeard; the isle is full of noises,
Sounds, and sweet airs, that give delight, and hurt not.

76.2   Close-up of Caliban's grinning face.

PROSPERO (playing Caliban):
Sometimes a thousand twangling instruments
Will hum about mine ears;

76.3   Close-up of the benign, smiling, Sphinx-like Ariel.

PROSPERO (playing Caliban):
. . . and sometime voices,
That, if I then had waked after long sleep,
Will make me sleep again: and then, in dreaming,
The clouds methought would open, and show riches . . .

76.4   Wide shot. Symmetrically placed – Caliban and Ariel in the centre of the picture – Trinculo and Stephano lying and squatting fearfully on the floor – their bodies sprawled in abject and almost

indecent postures – tangled up in yards and yards of Ariel's shining crimson ribbon. Now golden beams of light flash like bright night-time floodlights as the music continues to swirl stereophonically around them.

PROSPERO (playing Caliban):
. . . Ready to drop upon me; that, when I waked,
I cried to dream again.

Stephano – an abject, cowering figure – with his courage slowly returning.

PROSPERO (playing Stephano):
This will prove a brave kingdom to me, where I
shall have my music for nothing.

Caliban – grinning . . . and then serious –
76.5   Large close-up of Caliban's face.

PROSPERO (playing Caliban):
When Prospero is destroyed!

ACT III SCENE III
SECTION 77
THE PYRAMID

77.1   A view from the balcony of the island's pyramids – backed by the obelisks and the tall trees of the far forest. The camera takes flight – like a bird – and flies towards the largest of the pyramids . . . towards a rectangular black opening on its south-facing flank . . . into which it flies . . . then, to the long, sad strikes of a sonorous bell – we watch Prospero slowly walk out of the dark depth of the hole to approach its rim and catch the strong vertical golden sunlight of a stormy afternoon. Distant thunder rumbles.

The dark opening is flanked by Roman entabulature and surrounded by Latin inscriptions and symbols in the Rosicrucian manner. Prospero, wrapped in his (light blue) magic cloak – his head and hands showing – sits at the aperture and looks down. The camera follows his gaze downwards, and descends and retreats symmetrically – looking at the inscriptions, the tablets and the stone-cuttings on the pyramid's flank . . . to find a heavy symmetrical doorway which is closed . . . and to reveal at the base of the pyramid Alonso, Sebastian, Antonio, Gonzalo, Adrian, Francisco. They sit and stand on a flagged and decorated marble floor – marked out with the lines of old foundations.

PROSPERO (playing Alonso):
He is drowned,
Whom thus we stray to find; and the sea mocks
Our frustrate search on land. Well, let him go.

Whilst Alonso pathetically mumbles and mourns – Antonio and Sebastian – with nods and winks – indicate a return to their old plotting over his head. The camera continues to track down until it views the scene from ground-level.

To the sound of sonorous music and more bells, as we watch Alonso's company, the large metal doors of the pyramid open and a company of mythological figures carry out a large table . . . and tablecloths laden with food, wine and cornucopias of eatables that flutter with petals and butterflies, silverware, glassware . . . they pile high a table with a splendid banquet worthy of Veronese. They indicate that the party should eat . . . and then they retreat back into the pyramid . . . the sonorous bell stops and distant music plays quietly . . . small eddies and whirlpools of breeze spiral the petals upwards, and the atmosphere is one of great ominous silence . . . a melancholic ennui . . . a pause before violence.

It is very quiet . . . the camera gently moves in over the seated figure of Alonso to examine this munificent table; it silently examines the extravagant bounty.

Alonso and his crowd stare at the feast and begin to move towards it.

PROSPERO (playing Sebastian):
Now I will believe
That there are unicorns.
(playing Antonio):
Travellers ne'er did lie,
Though fools at home condemn 'em.

(playing Gonzalo):
If in Naples
I should report this now, would they believe me?

77.2   Up in his eyrie, Prospero is sitting regally . . . and in his lap – like a small white faun – sits Ariel, curled up – white, naked, chubby, innocence personified.
Prospero whispers in his ear . . . and gently stands Ariel on the lip of the void – Ariel makes ready to leap into the void like a swimmer about to dive into deep water . . . his toes curled around the lip-edge, his arms held back in preparation for a swallow-dive.
77.3   Down below, in front of the pyramid doors, the company approach the lavish meal set out on the table.

PROSPERO (playing Sebastian):
Will't please you taste of what is here?
(playing Alonso):
Not I.
(playing Gonzalo):
Faith, sir, you need not fear. When we were boys,
Who would believe that there were mountaineers
Dew-lapped like bulls, whose throats had hanging at 'em
Wallets of flesh? or that there were such men
Whose heads stood in their breasts?

Sebastian and Antonio step forward, the first to stretch out their hands to eat.
There is a great crash – the mechanical droning we associate with Prospero's magic – there is thunder and lightning and ear-splitting musical effects with great rhythmic insistency. The hands of Sebastian and Antonio are blackened. The air is full of whirling black feathers, the iron doors of the pyramid flap back and forth like crashing gongs, the munificence of the table turns to smoking ashes and cinders and black smoke . . . and Ariel – screaming and screeching like a harpy – clothed in black feathers – crashes onto the centre of the table from above . . . accompanied by seven black, reptilian fauns – all horns and feathers and sexual parts.

PROSPERO (playing Ariel):
You are three men of sin, whom Destiny –
That hath to instrument this lower world,
And what is in't – the never surfeited sea
Hath caused to belch up you; and on this island,
Where man doth not inhabit – you 'mongst men
Being most unfit to live.

77.4   In his eyrie in the pyramid up above – Prospero is on his feet and angrily declaiming. His voice – as Ariel – changes to his voice as himself.

At his back – a dim and shadowy mirror-image – carried by more black reptilian forms – demonstrates his threat.
Six men representing Alonso and his company – naked, bloodied, muddied and with wild hair – fall hanged from an invisible gallows.

PROSPERO:
I have made you mad;
And even with such-like valour, men hang and drown
Their proper selves.

MANIPULATING HIS BLACKENED, SCREECHING SPIRITS FROM HIS PYRAMID EYRIE, PROSPERO
CURSES HIS ENEMIES.

THE NEAPOLITAN CONSPIRATORS STAND SCOLDED AND SPELL-STOPPED BEFORE THE WRATH
OF PROSPERO'S FURIES.

77.5 On the ground, the company have drawn their swords. Feathers and soot fall like snow, and black water gushes around their feet – streaming out of the pyramid's double doors. Ariel and his reptilian companions continue to dance on the charred table.

PROSPERO (playing Ariel):
You fools! I and my fellows
Are ministers of Fate: the elements,
Of whom your swords are tempered, may as well
Wound the loud winds, or with bemocked-at stabs

Kill the still-closing waters, as diminish
One dowle that's in my plume: my fellow-ministers
Are like invulnerable. If you could hurt,
Your swords are now too massy for your strengths,
And will not be uplifted.

77.6 With Prospero up above.

PROSPERO:
But, remember –
For that's my business to you – that you three
From Milan did supplant good Prospero:

130

A mirror-image behind Prospero shows the image that we saw before of Prospero and Miranda abandoned on the ocean (Shot 34.37).

PROSPERO:
. . . Exposed unto the sea, which hath requit it,
Him and his innocent child: for which foul deed
The powers, delaying, not forgetting, have
Incensed the seas and shores, yea, all the creatures,
Against your peace.

77.7   A medium close-up of the dancing, raging, screeching Ariel behaving like a harpy.
PROSPERO (playing Ariel):
Thee of thy son, Alonso,
They have bereft; and do pronounce by me,
Ling'ring perdition – worse than any death
Can be at once – shall step by step attend
You and your ways; whose wraths to guard you from –
Which here, in this most desolate isle, else falls
Upon your heads – is nothing but heart-sorrow,
And a clear life ensuing.

Ariel and his minions disappear with a sudden and loud clattering of wings. To mock Alonso's grief . . . the loud tolling bell resumes . . . accompanied by ironic funereal organ music.
The table continues to smoke . . . in the smoke we can glimpse six funereal spirits – partially clothed in black and grey . . . with ash-smudged faces . . . carrying the naked, drenched, muddied, drowned body of Ferdinand. As the grey pall of smoke disperses . . . so do the funereal figures . . . Red-hot ashes glow where there was once drink and food, flowers and fine plate.
The camera slowly circles ninety degrees to observe Alonso. He weeps and sinks to his knees in the blackened, muddy sludge that covers the ground and which still flows out of the pyramid . . . it is like the aftermath of an earthquake . . . of a volcanic eruption. Alonso curls up with grief . . . his shoulders shake . . . he sobs pitifully . . . till his hands and arms are submerged in the mud . . . and his hair becomes matted with the sludge . . . finally his brow touches the ooze.

PROSPERO (playing Alonso):
O, it is monstrous, monstrous!
Methought the billows spoke, and told me of it;
The winds did sing it to me; and the thunder,
That deep and dreadful organ-pipe, pronounced
The name of Prosper: it did bass my trespass.
Therefore my son i' the ooze is bedded; and
I'll seek him deeper than e'er plummet sounded,
And with him there lie mudded.

77.7

ALONSO, FEARING THE VERY WORST FOR HIS SON AND HEIR, IS PERSUADED THAT FERDINAND IS DROWNED.

The flow stops, and the mud bubbles and steams and smokes like volcanic lava . . . Alonso sits – a miserable, wretched, suffering figure, kneeling in a pool of stagnant, oily, petrol-glazed ooze, his exquisite finery soiled. Beside him – in the mud . . . is materialised, spreadeagled, the naked, contorted – one leg bent under – wild-eyed corpse of his drowned son. There are bloodied wounds on his body, blood in his mouth.

Thus has Prospero's revenge been made horribly manifest.

Revenge is sweetest when it is savoured cold.

SECTION 78
PROSPERO'S STUDY

78.1 In his study . . . a little stunned at the revenge he is perpetrating on his enemies . . . since he – being a father – can understand Alonso's pain . . . Prospero sits, hunched – not unlike Alonso – over his desk . . . over the last words he has written . . . the last words spoken by Alonso. The pen is held aloft in his hand. He slowly mouths the words in a scarcely audible whisper.

PROSPERO:
I'll seek him deeper than e'er plummet sounded,
And with him there lie mudded.

Suddenly . . . to rudely break the reverie . . . Ariel . . . in a fall of black crow's feathers . . . his nakedness covered in soot and lamp-black – with a few black feathers still stuck to his body . . . falls onto the open white pages of Prospero's book. He smudges the pages.

Prospero starts and pulls himself together. To hide his hesitation, he plucks a few remaining feathers from Ariel's flesh. He speaks for the things that Ariel has performed have been performed at his, Prospero's, merciless command.

PROSPERO:
Bravely the figure of this harpy hast thou
Performed, my Ariel; a grace it had, devouring.
Of my instruction hast thou nothing bated
In what thou hadst to say: so, with good life
And observation strange, my meaner ministers
Their several kinds have done.

78.2 Ariel stands, leaving the black sooted imprint of his hands and buttocks – and now feet – on the clean white pages of the open book.

As we watch . . . a ripple of light wipes Ariel clean of soot.

78.3 A close-up of Prospero – willing himself to feel victorious – but noticeably equivocal about his revengeful plans now that they are being put into operation.

PROSPERO:
My high charms work,
And these mine enemies are all knit up
In their distractions: they now are in my power.

78.4 Suddenly standing, Prospero scoops Ariel up in his (light blue) cloak and prepares to leave his study. Ariel immediately struggles and flies up into the raftered ceiling of the library . . . out of Prospero's arms – like a pigeon thankfully escaped . . . a wind blows the pages of the *Tempest* book where Prospero has been writing . . . the pen rolls down the desk, splattering black ink . . .

78.5   The pen rolls off the desk and impales itself into the wooden floor . . . ink continues to magically flood off its nib . . .

78.6   Prospero's usual control is momentarily lost – he looks surprised and crestfallen . . . at Ariel's unaccustomed escape and at the pen that has also symbolically deserted him . . .

78.7   . . . The black ink turns to milk . . .

78.8   . . . which is licked up by the lion.

A C T   I V   S C E N E   I
SECTION 79
THE LIBRARY ATRIUM

79.1   The colour and lighting for this section is the very distinctive black, white and grey of the Laurenziana Atrium with strong, cool, white, vertical light bearing down on the action and characters – like strong, white light down a lift-shaft. The small, cubic, black, white and grey space is lit alternately by grey shadow and bright, white sunlight as clouds pass over the sun . . . though we cannot see the sky.

On the steps leading up to the main library, Ferdinand – like Christ in a Spanish Pietà – naked and bruised . . . his only garment, a loincloth like those worn by the crucified thieves in early Netherlandish crucifixions – is sprawled on the steps . . . his long black hair stuck to his forehead with sweat – there are twigs and bark-fragments from the woodyard in his hair – his hands and feet are scratched and bleeding, his white torso and belly are scratched and grimy. It is a grim image . . . another savage indication of vengeance and power which is dark and pitiful and ambiguous in its sexuality – Prospero's plans of revenge have again been realised.

Miranda – dressed in white, off-white and grey (in acknowledgement of the setting) walks quickly down the steps and – like the Virgin in a Pietà – sits and cradles Ferdinand's head in her lap. Despite her alarm . . . she is interested in his body. He is too exhausted to reciprocate.

As the camera – standing in for us and for Prospero – advances on the two figures symmetrically arranged on the stairs, Miranda wrenches her attention away from Ferdinand and, helping him to sit up – leaves him and comes down the steps to meet her father.

PROSPERO (off-screen voice):
If I have too austerely punished you,
Your compensation makes amends; for I
Have given you here a third of mine own life . . .

This metaphor – of thirds – is dramatically illustrated by Prospero's magic . . . Milan, Scholarship and Miranda – with the sudden appearance of two pyramidal or conical piles of items and Miranda herself . . . arranged symmetrically across the wide screen in front of the steps with the isolated Ferdinand behind. To contrast with the black-and-white setting, the objects in the conical piles are brightly coloured – predominantly orange, scarlet and sky-blue.

The conical pile on the left represents Milan. As tall as Miranda – it consists of piled charts and street-plans, crowns, keys of the city, ensigns, flags, banners, decorative armour, money in coins and bullion-bags, sealed documents and bonds, surmounted by a finely-made wooden model of a city – Milan – more like San Gimignano – with tall towers and battlements. Maybe – to make the identity certain – we may need the word 'Milan' written on a curling scroll of parchment as in a Mantegna allegorical painting.

In the centre – acting as a fulcrum – is a pyramidal or conical pile representing Prospero's studies – mainly books and papers but including scientific instruments, astrolabes, orreries, sextants, globes, mathematical figures . . . and antiquities – small busts of poets and philosophers, obelisks, inscribed fragments etc. . . . .

Miranda – looking flushed and beautiful – is standing on the right. As the two piles materialise – Prospero's four dancers arrive to clothe Miranda in a brightly coloured – predominantly orange and sky-blue – lavishly decorated and embellished – cloak.

PROSPERO:
. . . Or that for which I live; who once again
I tender to thy hand: all thy vexations
Were but my trials of thy love, and thou
Hast strangely stood the test: here, afore Heaven,
I ratify this my rich gift.

Prospero touches Miranda's shoulder and the two conical piles – representing Prospero's Milan and Prospero's scholarship – disappear in a swirl of wind and dust . . . and Prospero's dancers step forward to Miranda and take off her orange and sky-blue cloak – she is dressed again in white, off-white and grey.

79.2 A close-up of Miranda – lit by a sudden white/golden beam from above – flushed and smiling – holding her hands to her breasts, whose flesh – Bernini-like – palpably swells between her fingers.

79.3 Close-up of Ferdinand – smiling in expectation.

PROSPERO:
O Ferdinand,
Do not smile at me that I boast her off,
For thou shalt find she will outstrip all praise,
And make it halt behind her.

79.4 Wide shot.

PROSPERO:
As my gift, and thine own acquisition
Worthily purchased, take my daughter.

Prospero firmly takes Miranda's hand from her breast and leads her towards Ferdinand, who comes down the steps to meet them – the long perspective of the Laurenziana Library behind him.

SECTION 80
PROSPERO'S STUDY
80.1 In contrast to the last, predominantly brightly-lit, black-and-white sequence, this section – in Prospero's study – is golden and dark – with Rembrandt-like chiaroscuro lighting.

Prospero, after putting on a pair of gloves – presses a catch in his especially-constructed bookshelves for the twenty-four books . . . and a panel slides back to reveal a small compartment and a small black book. He takes it out and opens it on top of the other books on his desk where he is writing the drama of *The Tempest*.

The book is a small, blackened and thumbed volume – *The Autobiographies of Pasiphae and Semiramis* – a pornography. The illustrations leave no ambiguity as to the book's content. The book is bound in black calfskin with damaged lead covers . . . the pages are grey-green with line-engravings in black, touched out in white – the pages of the book are scattered with a sludge-green powder and curled black hairs and stains of blood and other substances.

The slightest taint of steam or smoke rises from the pages. As Prospero turns the dark pages they leave stains on his gloves – like the stains made by acid.

80.2 Prospero looks up from the volume before him to stare fiercely into space . . . and with much vehemence, he speaks aloud.

PROSPERO:
If thou dost break her virgin-knot before
All sanctimonious ceremonies may
With full and holy rite be ministered,
No sweet aspersion shall the heavens let fall
To make this contract grow;

80.3 Wide shot. To illustrate his words, lewd mythological figures dance around his desk – diseased, ape-like fauns, skinny witches waving bloodstained sheets, fighting harridans with snake-like hair. They are dusted in the same sludge-green powder as was found in the book . . . with their sexual characteristics provocatively reddened.

PROSPERO:
Sour-eyed disdain and discord shall bestrew
The union of your bed with weeds so loathly
That you shall hate it both:

SECTION 81
THE LIBRARY ATRIUM

81.1 Back in the very black-and-white atrium space – on the atrium steps – the four hand-maidens Miranda once talked of (from her childhood in Milan) – Prospero's dancers – are there with towels and scented water. Miranda washes Ferdinand's body with a sponge – her hands straying to his belly.

PROSPERO (voice off):
. . . therefore take heed,
As Hymen's lamps shall light you.

Behind the lovers at the top of the library steps . . . are mythological figures – brightly coloured in contrast to the black-and-white setting – waiting impatiently to perform in the coming masque . . . for, despite all Prospero's warnings – his blessing will be forthcoming – and his minions are eager to perform the betrothal celebrations like over-excited actors anxious to step onto the stage. The mythological figures of Iris and her companions are partly glimpsed at the door of the library – arranging their clothing.
The now naked Ferdinand takes the sponge from Miranda and turns his back to wash himself . . . she stands ready with his clothes.
The movement of towels and servants often masks Ferdinand's face, so that Prospero – speaking for him – has no trouble putting the words into his mouth. (As it is, Ferdinand's words are also seen – written on the white page – in Prospero's study – as Prospero conceives them.)

PROSPERO (playing Ferdinand):
As I hope
For quiet days, fair issue, and long life,
With such love as 'tis now, the murkiest den . . .

The same lewd creatures that had circled Prospero at his writing desk now appear in the library doorway . . .

. . . The most opportune place, the strong'st suggestion
Our worser genius can, shall never melt

Mine honour into lust, to take away
The edge of that day's celebration,
When I shall think, or Phoebus' steeds are foundered,
Or Night kept chained below.

The lewd figures are replaced by two large white horses that stand in the library doorway. And then . . . a dark figure – Night – a Herculean physique – bound with black chains.

PROSPERO:
Fairly spoke.
Sit, then, and talk with her; she is thine own.
What, Ariel! my industrious servant, Ariel!

Prospero walks up the steps – past the lovers . . . and on into the long library.

SECTION 82
THE LAURENZIANA LIBRARY

82.1 The library – in contrast to the black-and-white atmosphere of the atrium – is warmer and more golden-coloured – though not so golden or so dark as Prospero's study – it is a halfway stage between the two extremes . . .
A wide shot looking down the length of the library (in deep perspective) – tables, lecterns . . . rows and rows of books.
As Prospero calls for Ariel . . . there is a sudden great crash and a flash of light . . . and a smiling Ariel and a crowd of maenads, sirens, nymphs hamadryads and cherubs . . . (many of the characters in the coming masque) . . . drop from the library ceiling . . . in a fall of petals and flowers, sequins and sparks, scent, mist, steam, butterflies and coloured smoke. It is a multi-coloured crowd that favours flesh colours and pink and crimson.

PROSPERO:
Thou and thy meaner fellows your last service
Did worthily perform; and I must use you
In such another trick.

As the camera stays watching Ariel . . . Prospero, brisk and businesslike . . . like a schoolmaster

in a hurry ... sets off down the library to the other end ... swiftly and without stopping, rearranging a pile of books here ... sweeping a pile of petals off a table to the floor there ... talking over his shoulder.

PROSPERO:
Go, bring the rabble,
O'er whom I give thee power,
Incite them to quick motion; for I must
Bestow upon the eyes of this young couple
Some vanity of mine Art: it is my promise,
And they expect it from me.
(playing Ariel):
Presently?
PROSPERO (calling back along the library):
Ay, with a twink.

Ariel – standing on a table – surrounded by his 'rabble' – sings.

ARIEL:
Before you can say, 'come,' and 'go,'
And breathe twice, and cry, 'so, so,'
Each one, tripping on his toe,
Will be here with mop and mow.

82.2 At Prospero's end of the library – as Ariel sings – Prospero looks for a book along the shelves and – having selected one which is held down with a heavy brass weight, lifts the weight aside, takes the book down off the shelf and flips it open.

82.3 Close-up. Prospero turns the pages. It is *The Book of Motion* which, at its most simple level, describes how birds fly and waves roll, how clouds form and apples fall from trees. At its most complex level it explains how ideas chase one another in the memory and where thought goes when it is finished with. The book is covered in tough blue leather and, because it is always bursting open of its own volition, it is bound around with two leather straps buckled tightly at the spine. At night, it drums against the bookcase shelf and has to be held down with a brass weight.

One of its sections is called 'The Dance of Nature', and here, codified and explained in moving drawings, are all the possibilities for dance in the human body. The figures in the book dance about in vigorous animation.

82.4 At the other end of the library, Ariel finishes ... and calls out to Prospero – who, book in hand – is looking down the library at Ariel.

PROSPERO (playing Ariel):
Do you love me, master? no?

Prospero calls back along the length of the library.

PROSPERO:
Dearly, my delicate Ariel.

PROSPERO:

Look thou be true; do not give dalliance
Too much the rein: the strongest oaths are straw
To the fire i' the blood; be more abstemious.
Or else, good night your vow!

The lovers look suitably chastened. They sit . . . on a couch that is swiftly brought in for them – a formal day-bed with the sense of two separated chairs co-joined – like a domestic double throne.

Prospero claps his hands once. The clap echoes and grows rapidly into the magical drone that accompanies his magic. Rapidly a series of seven curtains peel back – the seven colours of Prospero's cloak – black, dark brown, dark blue, light blue, purple, dark red and fiery red . . . exposing more and more 'rabble' now disciplined into the masque attendants. The last curtain peels back to reveal the figure of Iris, the personification of the rainbow.

IN THE CERTAIN HOPE OF DYNASTIC SUCCESSION IN THE HOUSES OF MILAN AND NAPLES, PROSPERO UNITES FERDINAND AND MIRANDA.

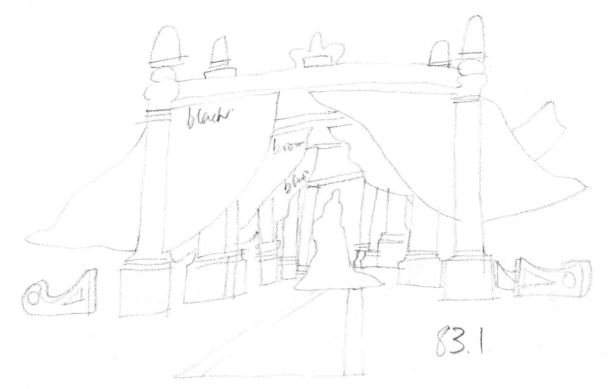

THE MASQUE

The masque is created by a great company – the mythological spirits of Prospero's island – who – through Prospero's learning and Renaissance interests – he has conceived of as being Hellenic-Roman – the Olympian creatures we have seen much of. The 'John White' Indian-natives are also present – both contributing action and also being spectators . . .

Since the spirits have been much in evidence already – their contributions – through the masque – must be particular to retrieve the impact they would have had in a more conventional theatrical performance of the play where their presence – though hinted at – has never been allowed to flourish until this moment in the narrative. Prospero's 'personal' dancers lead the whole troupe . . . and the music is stately, grand and very 'civilised', as becomes a chaste wedding celebration . . . but not without irony – for we can suppose that – as already evidenced – the spirits of the island have an existence of their own which is given to ribaldry – remembering their origins and Caliban's remark that they would behave very dif-

ferently if Prospero's power declined. Iris and Ceres sing.

This whole section would be best choreographed by a professional choreographer/dancer in collaboration with the demands of the music which should be pre-composed and – at least in part – recorded and rough-mixed for good playback.

IRIS:

Ceres, most bounteous lady, thy rich leas
Of wheat, rye, barley, vetches, oats, and pease;
Thy turfy mountains, where live nibbling sheep,
And flat meads thatched with stover, them to keep;
Thy banks with pioned and twilled brims,
Which spongy April at thy hest betrims,
To make cold nymphs chaste crowns; and thy
   broom-groves,
Whose shadow the dismissed bachelor loves,
Being lass-lorn; thy poss-clipt vineyard;
And thy sea-marge, sterile and rocky-hard,
Where thou thyself dost air – the queen o' the sky,
Whose wat'ry arch and messenger am I,
Bids thee leave these; and with her sovereign grace,

PROSPERO IN HIS LIBRARY CONSULTS THE BOOK OF MOTION BEFORE ORDERING THE
BETROTHAL ENTERTAINMENTS.

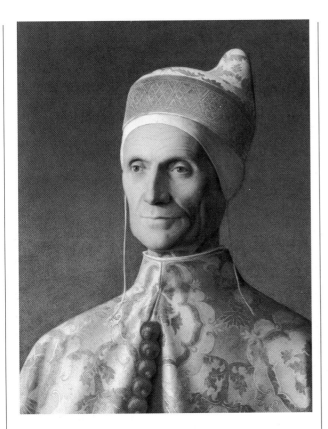

PROSPERO DRESSES AS A VENETIAN DOGE, TRADITIONAL ENEMY OF MILAN AND SYMBOL OF JEALOUSLY GUARDED PRIVILEGE AND RUTHLESS MARITIME AUTHORITY.

82.5 From Prospero's point-of-view looking back down the length of the library towards Ariel standing on the table.

PROSPERO:
Do not approach
Till thou dost hear me call.

Prospero puts the book – *The Book of Motion* – back on the shelf . . .

82.6 The book immediately begins to jump and vibrate on the shelf – Prospero turns the book on its side and holds it down with the brass weight.

82.7 Prospero leaves the library. We wait – looking down the length of the library at Ariel and the large troupe – his 'rabble' – who are crowding – silently – through the doors behind him. Then a loud echoic shout from Prospero – off-screen.

PROSPERO:
Now come, my Ariel!

At once – Ariel leads his skittering 'rabble' down the library towards the camera . . . a crowd of two hundred – containing creatures of very different sizes . . . giant Amazons with small pygmies . . . maenads, fauns, nymphs, cupids, sirens . . . leaping over and under and around the tables of books . . . a bacchanalian host – carrying all the materials and props for a masque or play . . . curtains, banners, flags, garlands, laurel wreaths, ribbons, fruit, flowers, baskets of petals, armour, costumes, helmets, jugs, screens, ropes, mirrors, torches, lamps, animals, skins . . . etc.

All these objects are brightly coloured with the colouring and texture of varnished objects – masks that are crimson-laquered, armour that is silver-chased on gold on a black patina-ed base, fruit that looks almost waxen with a high shine, laurel wreaths that are interlaced with red lacquered berries, white flowers and small oranges.

SECTION 83
THE GARDEN

83.1 The lovers are standing in front of Prospero in a garden. Behind them – Ariel's host are preparing for a masque. The light-scheme of things is here becoming much more complex. It is magical as befits a masque. There is still a strong sense of top-lighting – which is now predominantly golden, but the skies are darkening into a flaring red-and-orange sunset and there is much use of artificial lights being lit – lamps and torches and flares.

Curtains are being swiftly hung . . . the four accompanying dancers are providing a prologue – whilst Prospero and the lovers in the centre foreground are strongly lit.

CERES, SUMMONED TO BLESS THE UNION OF MIRANDA AND FERDINAND, PREPARES THEM TO MEET JUNO AND CELEBRATE THE BETROTHAL.

Juno descends.

Here, on this grass-plot, in this very place,
To come and sport: her peacocks fly amain;
Approach, rich Ceres, her to entertain.

Enter Ceres

CERES:
Hail, many-coloured messenger, that ne'er
Dost disobey the wife of Jupiter;

142

Who, with thy saffron wings, upon my flowers
Diffusest honey-drops, refreshing showers;
And with each end of thy blue bow dost crown
My bosky acres, and my unshrubbed down,
Rich scarf to my proud earth; why hath thy Queen
Summoned me hither, to this short-grassed green?
IRIS:
A contract of true love to celebrate;
And some donation freely to estate
On the blest lovers.
CERES:
Tell me, heavenly bow,
If Venus or her son, as thou dost know,
Do now attend the Queen? Since they did plot
The means that dusky Dis my daughter got,
Her and her blind boy's scandaled company
I have forsworn.
IRIS:
Of her society
Be not afraid: I met her deity
Cutting the clouds towards Paphos, and her son
Dove-drawn with her. Here thought they to have done
Some wanton charm upon this man and maid,
Whose vows are, that no bed-right shall be paid
Till Hymen's torch be lighted: but in vain;
Mars's hot minion is returned again;
Her waspish-headed son has broke his arrows,
Swears he will shoot no more, but play with sparrows,
And be a boy right out.
CERES:
Highest Queen of state,
Great Juno comes.
JUNO:
How does my bounteous sister? Go with me,
To bless this twain, that they may be prosperous be,
And honoured in their issue.

They sing.

JUNO:
Honour, riches, marriage-blessing,
Long continuance, and increasing,
Hourly joys be still upon you!
Juno sings her blessings on you.

CERES:
Earth's increase, foison plenty,
Barns and garners never empty;
Vines with clustering bunches growing;
Plants with goodly burthen bowing;
Spring come to you at the farthest
In the very end of harvest!
Scarcity and want shall shun you;
Ceres' blessing so is on you.
FERDINAND:
Let me live here ever;
So rare a wondered father and a wise
Makes this place Paradise.
IRIS:
You nymphs, called Naiads, of the windring brooks,
With your sedged crowns and ever-harmless looks,
Leave your crisp channels, and on this green land
Answer your summons; Juno does command:
Come, temperate nymphs, and help to celebrate
A contract of true love; be not too late.

The wedding vows are celebrated . . .

THE BETROTHAL OF FERDINAND AND MIRANDA IS CELEBRATED WITH AN ENTERTAINMENT
PERFORMED BY THE ISLAND'S SPIRITS.

The hall fills with dancers.

83.2   Medium close-up. Prospero starts suddenly
. . . he stands up in consternation – worried,
anxious, angry. There is a rapidly growing roar – a
threatening noise – the approach of his magic – his
cloak begins to glow red. Behind him, the company
of the masque freeze and grow anxious. The
golden top-light darkens. After a confused
moment:

PROSPERO (with great anger):
I had forgot that foul conspiracy . . .

83.3   Wide shot. Facing the masque – with

Miranda and Ferdinand in the middle-ground
behind Prospero. Prospero turns his back on the
masque to face the camera. Behind and to both
sides of Prospero, three sets of mirror bearers
appear in the dim light carrying speckled mirrors
in which flicker the images of the Antonio plot
against his life in Milan twelve years previously.

Reprint previous shots:
Shot 34.9: Antonio's men plotting.
Shot 34.18: Milanese political prisoners in chains.
Shot 34.21: Antonio's bath-house sequence with
Alonso.

Shot 34.23: The marching feet of Antonio's soldiers.
Shot 34.25: The ravaged dormitory in Milan.
Shot 34.26: Prospero dragged out of bed.
Shot 34.28: Miranda lifted from her cradle.

PROSPERO:
. . . Of the beast Caliban and his confederates
Against my life.

The company are all looking anxiously in Prospero's direction.

PROSPERO:
Our revels now are ended. These our actors,
Were all spirits, and are melted into air,
Into thin air . . .

83.4   A montage. The masque and its company begin to dissolve.
(1) Characters in the masque – freeze and turn into whitened versions of themselves . . . a white dust falls on them.
(2) An acrobatic quartet of garlanded dancers freeze and dissolve.
(3) Three characters in a group crumple and fall to the ground like old clothes.
(4) Close-up of the faces of four dancers who fade into hair and paper masks.
(5) Silk banners are rippled off a podium, scattering flower-heads.
(6) Four characters dancing off to the left freeze in a statuesque pose and fade away.
(7) An archway decorated with flowers and ribbons – in slow-motion – begins to topple . . . fruit scattering.
(8) Book pages whirl away in a sudden gust of wind.
(9) Close-up of a bunch of flowered garlands withering to greyness.
(10) Costumes are thrown into a hamper.
(11) An orange-bush is shaken and all the oranges fall off.
(12) Fingers pinch out decorated candles.
(13) Five fauns hurriedly roll up a large flag.
(14) Five spirits quickly untie masks and throw them in a trunk and slam the lid.

(15) Five dryads roll up a carpet.
(16) In slow-motion – swathes of red ribbon fall to the floor.
(17) A party of eight dancers stripped to the skin.
(18) A section of flower-strewn grass turns white in a gust of wind.
(19) Six masque-players drag a painted canvas across the grass – with two young fauns sitting on the canvas.
(20) A de la Tour-lit girl blows out a candle.
(21) An orange-bush in a tub is wheeled away in a barrow.
(22) A length of carpet on the grass is scattered with charcoal.
(23) A pan of salt is thrown on a brazier – its flames turn yellow and go out.
(24) A young faun blows out a candle.
(25) Water is thrown on a brazier – it spits steam and blackens.
(26) A black rain falls – staining white sheets carried by children.
(27) Grey smoke blows across a party of dancers carrying away props.
(28) A very young child blows out a candle.
The activity continues as Prospero describes the collapse of the play.

83.5   Wide shot. The curtains are drawn . . . each painted curtain shows an image we have seen before . . . the bath-house, the library, the beach, the forest . . .

PROSPERO:
. . . And, like the baseless fabric of this vision,
The cloud-capped towers, the gorgeous palaces,
The solemn temples, the great globe itself,
Yea, all which it inherit, shall dissolve,
And, like this insubstantial pageant faded,
Leave not a rack behind.

The final curtain is pulled across – the play has ended, the stage is bare . . . the rain falls, the wind blows.
Prospero, with his back to the curtains and the stage, speaks to the lovers and, over their heads, to us, the audience.

PROSPERO:
We are such stuff
As dreams are made on; and our little life
Is rounded with a sleep.

83.6 Prospero in close-up – he closes his eyes.
83.7 Miranda and Ferdinand look on anxiously as the foreground curtains close . . . through them slips an angelic figure with a six-branched candelabrum.
Whilst Prospero stands – in the gloom – with his eyes closed . . . the angel conducts the lovers away. Prospero's face is slowly lost in the disappearing light of the angel's golden candles.

SECTION 84
PROSPERO'S STUDY
84.1 Ariel sits on a pile of open books on Prospero's desk . . . in the attitude of his painted image on the curtain.

PROSPERO:
Spirit,
We must prepare to meet with Caliban.

Prospero swishes back a heavy embroidered curtain in his study to reveal large cupboard doors we had not suspected – which open inwards to reveal racks and pegs and shelves . . . which, by a mechanism, push or swing forward – to exhibit rows and rows of clothes – rich finery like that worn by Alonso and his company – circular ruffs, circular hats, square cloaks, rectangular sashes, swords, buckled shoes – all arranged neatly for their geometric effect. The four women (the dancers) who attended Miranda appear and – directed by Ariel – take what he swiftly pulls down from the shelves.

SECTION 85
THE CANAL
85.1 A virtuoso, bravura travelling shot. With the camera close to the ground . . . down a gloomy, sloping tunnel of vegetation in the forest – looped and thorned briars, fallen trees – the whole lit by a brown, vertical, dappled top-light the camera retreats before Caliban, Trinculo and Stephano who walk quickly – their faces upturned to catch what light there is. They are drawn by music that is ever before them. Their faces are ripped and torn, what is left of their clothing is muddied and bloodied. The gloomy tunnel gets darker and darker. There are blue phosphorescent fireflies and hybrid-animals like ambiguous, blue-banded, long-snouted pigs that rush away from their stumbling approach. Horned and winged children and dark shaggy fauns disappear into the brambles – the spirits that Prospero has relegated to the gloom.
The camera continues to retreat until the ground gets swampy . . . and the trio splash in and out of puddles . . . until suddenly – with a stumbling cry . . . they all fall into chest-deep water in a canal of mud and silt . . . where obese mud-covered creatures with large breasts and red eyes splash and wallow.
Still with the camera retreating – and with a great

brown darkness about them . . . they trip, stumble and wade – led by the music – into stretches of phosphorescent slime . . . coming at last to a flight of long broad steps . . . overhung by trees and vegetation and fallen architecture . . . up which they drag themselves . . . the black water running off their backs. They are confronted by a row of black, porphyry statues aranged at short intervals on squat pedestals along the canal-bank.

Beyond the steps, there are yet more steps and the suggestion of columns . . . we are close to the back of Prospero's bath-halls and near to the sump where Caliban lives.

PROSPERO (playing Caliban):
Pray you, tread softly, that the blind mole may not
Hear a foot fall: we now are near his cell.
(playing Trinculo):
Monster, I do smell all horse-piss; at which my nose is in
great indignation.
(playing Caliban):
Be patient, for the prize I'll bring thee to
Shall hoodwink this mischance: therefore speak softly.
All's hushed as midnight yet.

85.2 The statues are black-leaded and nakedly glistening – they are spirits – the slightest of movements give them away.

As the trio attempt to wash off the mud at a running spigot shaped like a large, grotesque mouth, Ariel, flying overhead unobserved – hangs the clothing he has brought from Prospero's study on the statues.

85.3 Medium shot of the conspirators – their heads together in the gloom.

PROSPERO (playing Caliban):
Prithee, my King, be quiet. See'st thou here,
This is the mouth o' the cell: no noise, and enter:
Do that good mischief which may make this island
Thine own for ever, and I, thy Caliban,
For aye thy foot-licker.
(playing Stephano):
Give me thy hand. I do begin to have bloody thoughts.

85.4 They climb the steps and discover the clothes. Trinculo and Stephano snatch them down from the statues and try to put them on.

PROSPERO (playing Trinculo):
O King Stephano! O peer! O worthy Stephano! look what
a wardrobe here is for thee!
(playing Caliban):
Let it alone, thou fool; it is but trash.
What do you mean
To dote thus on such luggage? Let't alone,
And do the murther first: if he awake,
From toe to crown he'll fill our skins with pinches,
Make us strange stuff.
(playing Stephano):
Be you quiet, monster.

85.5 Wide shot of the steps and the statues.

(playing Caliban):
We shall lose our time,
And all be turned to barnacles, or to apes
With foreheads villainous low.

Suddenly – to the accompaniment of Prospero's 'mechanical' pre-music noise – bright orange light floods down the steps as though a succession of wide doors have been thrown open . . . and thirty fierce dogs appear among the columns at the top of the steps – smooth-haired black dogs that – like the statues – have a marbled, black-leaded appearance. They all wear identical silver-spiked collars and are held on leashes by dimly-seen naked female forms – ten images of Diana the huntress . . . complete with arrows, longbows and quivers and the emblem of a silver moon that glints in the gloom.

Trinculo, Stephano and Caliban take flight. Wearing their finery, they splash back into the canal . . . the dogs are unleashed and race down the steps in pursuit.

85.6 Making the same travelling shot as before . . . but this time following on behind instead of retreating . . . and travelling much faster . . . the camera follows the fleeing trio . . . splashing back through the murky water – surrounded by the

147

obese and ambiguous water-spirits . . . scrambling out on the canal-bank . . . ripping through briars and back up the tunnel of overhead vegetation. The dogs in pursuit – baying and barking.

SECTION 86
THE 'ANTIQUARIAN' BEACH
86.1 The trio break from the forest – from screen left to right . . . and rush pell-mell through the 'antiquarian' ruins . . . the camera travelling alongside . . . with Ariel hovering overhead . . . the camera rises on a crane to meet up with Ariel . . . and watch the trio from above – running for their lives . . . shedding some of their finery, which is now ripped and torn and bloodied . . . and then the camera descends back to ground-level on the other side . . . to view them running from screen right to left.

SECTION 87
THE BEACH
87.1 A travelling shot – the trio – still casting off their bloodied finery . . . heavily panting in short gasps with the asthmatic breathing of the panic-stricken . . . rush across the empty ribbed sands and splash into the sea . . . the camera still following them . . . until they are waist-deep in the sea-water . . . washed and splashed by the surf . . . hugging on to one another and screaming themselves hoarse for a ship . . . the camera dispassionately turns ninety degrees to see the thirty snapping and snarling, barking and baying dogs on the sand . . . held by the ten Diana figures. Beyond – across the wide screen – there is an orange-and-black sunset silhouetting Prospero's palace – with a brightly/whitely-lit serene Ariel hovering in the very centre of the picture against the darkening sky . . . in the foreground the desperate, terrified figures of Trinculo, Stephano and Caliban.

This is another savage image of Prospero's revenge which is dark and pitiful . . . and makes Ariel ashamed.

SECTION 88
PROSPERO'S STUDY
88.1 In Prospero's study. Prospero is almost gleeful. Ariel stands on the desk before him – silent and straight-faced. Prospero's magic music winds down. Distant barking is still heard . . . and distant sobbing.
Prospero holds up his pen triumphantly.
He is pleased with himself and pleased with his writing.

PROSPERO:
At this hour
Lies at my mercy all mine enemies:
Shortly shall all my labours end, and thou
Shalt have the air at freedom.
Now does my project gather to a head:
My charms crack not; my spirits obey; and time
Goes upright with his carriage. Say, my spirit,
How fares the King and's followers?
ARIEL (finding – for the first time – his own voice):
Confined together
In the same fashion as you gave in charge,
Just as you left them; all prisoners, sir,

Prospero is taken aback. Ariel answers for the first time . . . and answers like a man forced to obey orders he does not approve of. He ventures the slightest of criticisms.

ARIEL:
Your charm so strongly works 'em,
That if you now beheld them, your affections
Would become tender.
PROSPERO:
Dost thou think so, spirit?
Dost thou think so, spirit?
Dost thou think so, spirit?

Prospero shakes Ariel with some anger . . . then, ashamed to see Ariel's stern face . . . with some guilt.
A turning point. Ariel – his creature – has spoken and has rebuked him.

THE FUTURE

The second part — the present — is over; all plans for revenge are superseded. The film now moves into scenes of night — a soft calm night with the aurora borealis, shooting stars, comets and a crescent moon . . . a night of forgiveness after the tumult of the bright-and-white toplight sections of the second part.

88.2

SECTION 88
PROSPERO'S STUDY

88.2 Prospero slumps back in his chair. Ariel brings on three mirror-images carried by draped figures . . .

(1) Alonso – a stricken father who has lost his son – weeping in the oily mud with his muddied, dead son beside him.

(2) The exhausted, brutalised body of Ferdinand on the steps of the library.

(3) The terrified trio of Caliban, Trinculo and Stephano standing shivering in the sea.

Ariel drops the bloodied finery that was worn by Trinculo and Stephano onto the desk on top of Prospero's book.

For the first time – Prospero – as writer of *The Tempest* – leaves his writing-study.

The camera turns forty-five degrees . . . so we can no longer see Ariel . . . and we watch Prospero as he walks up and down in his library – looking at the yellow ship outside his windows . . . pondering a change of heart. The mirror-bearers continue to hold up the images of revenge.

The camera swings back forty-five degrees to see that Ariel has been sitting writing at Prospero's desk.

88.3 A close-up. Ariel has written the last lines he spoke: 'Your charm so strongly works them, That if you now beheld them, your affections would become tender.'

88.4 Ariel puts down the pen and indicates that the mirror-carriers should depart – which they do. Prospero returns to his desk, reads the words and mouths them to himself. He draws in a breath and quietly says:

PROSPERO:
And mine shall.
Hast thou, which art but air, a touch, a feeling
Of their afflictions, and shall not myself,

150

One of their kind, that relish all as sharply
Passion as they, be kindlier moved than thou art?
Though with their high wrongs I am struck to the quick,
Yet with my nobler reason, 'gainst my fury
Do I take part: the rarer action is
In virtue than in vengeance: they being penitent,
The sole drift of my purpose doth extend
Not a frown further.

88.5   Close-up. Prospero flips shut the book of *The Tempest* . . .

88.6   Close-up. He snaps his pen.

88.7   Mid-shot. He closes all the books in his study . . . blows out the candles, picks up his staff/crozier . . . and leaves the study and closes its curtains.

88.8   Here begins a big set-piece. Prospero stands in front of the closed curtains in front of his large library and begins to walk forward through the book-laden tables and bookshelves . . . the camera retreats before him.

As he walks – so all the spirits . . . from nowhere – magicked out of thin air . . . out of the books . . . from under tables . . . from right and left . . . from the ceiling and the floorboards . . . gather in a crowd behind him. They scramble across the tables, push through among the books, come down off the walls, from out of the shelves and from behind bookcases.

As the camera retreats – its view of the library grows wider and wider – with Prospero always at its centre. Prospero's pre-music noise commences. His cloak begins to glow red.

As Prospero lists the various categories of his magic – so the various spirits appear out of thin air and the woodwork . . . and group themselves behind him – in order . . . the elves, nymphs and nereids, the sea-creatures and sirens, the fauns from orchards and harvests, the nocturnal spirits, the wind-spirits, the Olympian horde, and the dead – arising in shrouds – as though rising from coffins resting on the tables.

PROSPERO:
Ye elves of hills, brooks, standing lakes, and groves;

And ye that on the sands with printless foot
Do chase the ebbing Neptune, and do fly him
When he comes back; you demi-puppets that
By moonshine do the green sour ringlets make,
Whereof the ewe not bites; and you whose pastime
Is to make midnight mushrooms, that rejoice
To hear the solemn curfew; by whose aid –
Weak masters though ye be – I have bedimmed
The noontide sun, called forth the mutinous winds,
And 'twixt the green sea snd the azured vault
Set roaring war: to the dread rattling thunder
Have I given fire, and rifted Jove's stout oak
With his own bolt; the strong-based promontory
Have I made shake, and by the spurs plucked up
The pine and cedar: graves at my command
Have waked their sleepers, ope'd, and let 'em forth
By my so potent Art.

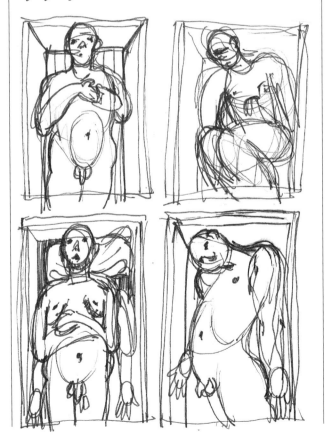

Prospero comes to a vast – wide and long –
table at the end of the library – covered in
instruments and books – a crowd of at least
two hundred spirits and mythological
creatures have formed up behind him –
on the tables, lecterns, flying in the air –
looking over his shoulder. He takes a
large pair of compasses – and like William
Blake's God – on a huge sheet of paper he
draws a circle – anticlockwise to camera.

WILLIAM BLAKE'S CHRONUS WITH HIS SET
OF COMPASSES DRAWING A MAGIC CIRCLE,
AN IMAGE OF PROSPERO PREPARING HIS
GEOMANCY TO ENSNARE HIS ENEMIES.

PROSPERO:
But this rough magic
I here abjure; and, when I have required
Some heavenly music – which even now I do –

With a crashing tumult . . . the Prospero drone
gives way to music.

PROSPERO:
To work mine end upon their senses, that
This airy charm is for, I'll break my staff,
Bury it certain fathoms in the earth,
And deeper than did ever plummet sound,
I'll drown my books.

With the sound of an enormous splash . . . and the
visual sensation of the shadow of a splash over the
library walls . . . and a great light . . . brighter than
the interior light in the library . . . flashing yellow
and white and orange outside . . . all the mythological creatures in the library vanish . . . leaving Prospero singularly illuminated in red against blackness . . . a majestic figure standing above his vast
drawn circle.

SECTION 89
THE QUINCUNX

89.1   To the growing crescendo of Prospero's music . . . in the grounds of the gathering of pyramids – symmetrically before the largest pyramid – there is a large, geometrically arranged plot of mixed sand and grass – under a quincunx of twenty-five heavily-laden orange-trees. The blinding white, revolving, bright light from the island lighthouse – from beyond the other side of the pyramids – throws the triangular shadows of all the pyramids across the quincunx.

As we watch, a large circle is miraculously drawn in fire and smoke (that blows to the right) – and corresponds exactly to the circle drawn by Prospero on the paper laid on the table in the Laurenziana library.

The camera angle of the quincunx and the table circles are identical and could be intercut. The circle is drawn anticlockwise, leaving an entrance-space at the pyramid side for the entry of Prospero's enemies.

The camera moves on a greater concentric circle on the outside of the quincunx and starts at a point to watch a flying Ariel push and pull the miscreants into the circle . . . dragging them on red ribbons that are caught about their arms, waists, shoulders . . .

The miscreants – Alonso, Sebastian, Antonio, Gonzalo, Adrian and Francisco – stumble, hesitate, resist – but to no avail. Once in – they stand charmed, and the camera begins to circle to a point to witness the arrival of Prospero, coming down a great avenue of heavily-laden orange-trees. When Prospero is close . . . Ariel twirls and turns the miscreants for Prospero's observation . . .

PROSPERO:
A solemn air, and the best comforter
To an unsettled fancy, cure thy brains,
Now useless, boiled within thy skull! There stand,
For you are spell-stopped.

89.2   The camera circles Gonzalo . . . watching Prospero circle the old man – circles within circles.

PROSPERO:
Holy Gonzalo, honourable man,
Mine eyes, ev'n sociable to the show of thine,
Fall fellowly drops. The charm dissolves apace:
And as the morning steals upon the night,
Melting the darkness, so their rising senses
Begin to chase the ignorant fumes that mantle
Their clearer reason. O good Gonzalo,
My true preserver, and a loyal sir
To him thou follow'st! I will pay thy graces
Home both in word and deed.

89.3   The camera circles Alonso and his brother, Sebastian.

PROSPERO:
Most cruelly
Didst thou, Alonso, use me and my daughter:
Thy brother was a furtherer in the act.
Thou art pinched for 't now, Sebastian.

153

89.4 The camera circles Antonio.

PROSPERO:
Flesh and blood,
You, brother mine, that entertained ambition,
Expelled remorse and nature; who, with Sebastian –
Whose inward pinches therefore are most strong –
Would here have killed your King; I do forgive thee,
Unnatural though thou art.

89.5 The whole circle is seen as the camera circles on the outer perimeter.

PROSPERO:
Their understanding
Begins to swell; and the approaching tide
Will shortly fill the reasonable shore
That now lies foul and muddy. Not one of them

That yet looks on me, or would know me: Ariel,
I will discase me, and myself present
As I was sometime Milan: quickly, spirit;
Thou shalt ere long be free.

89.6 Prospero is disrobed of his blue cloak which – carried by two hovering putti – is held aloft like the backcloth to a throne. In front of this rich and tasselled black cloth – hanging like a skin of office . . . Prospero is dressed by the four dancers who have always accompanied him . . . moving and dancing all the while to Ariel's music. The clothes he puts on are identical in style – but much more lavish – and befitting a Duke (and an elderly man) – as Alonso's. When he is dressed in costume – Prospero outshines Alonso and all the rest of the company.

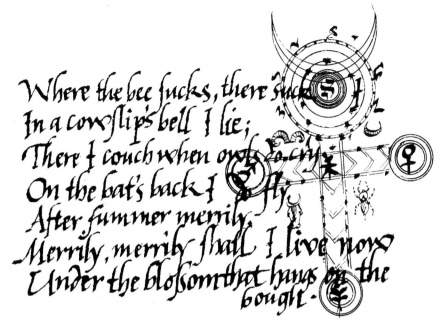

This dressing takes the time it needs . . .

89.7   . . . and is intercut with the camera swiftly sweeping around the outer concentric circle – concentrating on Ariel at the centre of its vision and interest. Ariel dances, flies and sings.

ARIEL:
Where the bee sucks, there suck I:
In a cowslip's bell I lie;
There I couch when owls do cry.
On the bat's back I do fly
After summer merrily.
Merrily, merrily shall I live now
Under the blossom that hangs on the bough.

To provide adequate time for the dressing – this piece can be sung twice or embellished to last at least two minutes.

89.8   Prospero continues to dress and be dressed.

PROSPERO:
Why, that's my dainty Ariel! I shall miss thee;
But yet thou shalt have freedom: so, so, so.
To the King's ship, invisible as thou art:
There shalt thou find the mariners asleep
Under the hatches; the master and the boatswain
Being awake, enforce them to this place,
And presently, I prithee.

89.9   Ariel runs and flies straight for

Prospero's hanging cloak . . . and bursts through it – turning it fiery red in a large O at its centre – but the cloak is unmarked – the large red O turns maroon, purple, blue, brown, and finally back to black.

89.9.

89.10 With a flourish of music and magic – Prospero presents himself as a regal Duke of Milan.

PROSPERO:
Behold, sir King,
The wronged Duke of Milan, Prospero:
For more assurance that a living Prince
Does now speak to thee, I embrace thy body;
And to thee and thy company I bid
A hearty welcome.

89.11 Circling around Alonso. Prospero's imaginings have created the characters, but it is only his forgiveness that has breathed life into them – they are now truly alive.

ALONSO (speaking in his own voice):
Whether thou be'st he or no,
Or some enchanted trifle to abuse me,
As late I have been, I not know; thy pulse
Beats, as of flesh and blood; and since I saw thee,
Th'affliction of my mind amends, with which,
I fear, a madness held me; this must crave –
An if this be at all – a most strange story.
Thy dukedom I resign, and do entreat
Thou pardon me my wrongs: but how should Prospero
Be living and be here?
PROSPERO:
First, noble friend,
Let me embrace thine age, whose honour cannot
Be measured or confined.
GONZALO: (Speaking in his own voice)
Whether this be
Or be not, I'll not swear.
PROSPERO:
You do yet taste
Some subtleties o' the isle, that will not let you
Believe things certain. Welcome, my friends all!
(Aside, to Sebastian and Antonio):
But you, my brace of lords, were I so minded
I here could pluck his highness' frown upon you,
And justify you traitors: at this time
I will tell no tales.
SEBASTIAN (Speaking in his own voice aside):
The devil speaks in him.

PROSPERO:
No. For you, most wicked sir, whom to call brother
Would even infect my mouth, I do forgive
Thy rankest fault – all of them – and require
My dukedom of thee, which perforce, I know,
Thou must restore.
ALONSO:
If thou be'st Prospero,
Give us particulars of thy preservation;
How thou hast met us here, whom three hours since
Were wracked upon this shore; where I have lost –
How sharp the point of this remembrance is! –
My dear son Ferdinand.
Irreparable is the loss; and patience
Says it is past her cure.
PROSPERO:
I rather think
You have not sought her help, of whose soft grace
For the like loss I have her sovereign aid,
And rest myself content.
ALONSO:
You the like loss?
PROSPERO:
As great to me, as late; and, supportable
To make the dear loss, have I means much weaker
Than you may call to comfort you, for I
Have lost my daughter.
ALONSO:
A daughter?
O heavens, that they were living both in Naples,
The King and Queen there! That they were, I wish
Myself were mudded in that oozy bed
Where my son lies. When did you lose your daughter?
PROSPERO:
Know for certain
That I am Prospero, and that very Duke
Which was thrust forth of Milan; who most strangely
Upon this shore, where you were wracked, was landed,
To be the lord on't.
This cell's my court: pray you, look in.
My dukedom since you have given me again,
I will requite you with as good a thing;
At least bring forth a wonder, to content ye
As much as me my dukedom.

156

TWO OF THE FOUR ARIELS WITH THE ALLEGORIES OF AUTUMN, INTRODUCE THE FINAL
BETROTHAL MASQUE.

From the front entrance of the pyramid . . . a crowd of spirits draws forth a complex of awnings and red varnished poles and scarlet banners . . . like a Renaissance marquee . . . and then by drawing back a succession of seven curtains – forever getting brighter and more colourful – black, brown, dark blue, light blue, purple, dark red and scarlet . . . the colours of Prospero's chameleon magic cloak . . . they flourish open the last curtain to discover in the portico of a lavish banqueting hall – Ferdinand and Miranda playing at chess. The two lovers are dressed in the manner of Alonso and his

company – but even more splendidly. They turn to face the company and they stand, smiling – a radiant pair in a radiant image.

89.12 The camera travels forward and moves in on the chess-board. Detail. *The Book of Games*. Some 80 by 40 by 25 centimetres. The chess-board is the double-page spread of a book. As we watch, the board begins to close like the turning of a page – the chess-pieces rolling away. Turning more of the stiff pages reveals a host of board games to be played with counters and dice, with cards and spinning-tops, flags and minute pyramids, pawns and chess-pieces, small figures of the Olympic gods, the winds in coloured glass, Old Testament prophets as marble statuettes, Roman busts, the oceans of the world, exotic animals, pieces of coral, gold putti, silver coins, pieces of exotic jewellery . . . and so on. The book is accompanied by an ornate redwood box containing the hundreds of different playing-pieces. The various board-games represented in the book cover many situations – gaming-boards of red and black triangles, grey and blue diamonds, boards in the shape of the constellations, animals, maps, the human body, journeys and so on.

89.13   Mid-shot. The book finally closes on all the board-games and retracts automatically into a finely crafted and veneered table. The clasped hands of Miranda and Ferdinand in a handshake that is indicative of their mutual affection but is also heraldic – an image of a dynastic union.

89.14   Alonso, surprised, shocked, startled.

ALONSO:
If this prove
A vision of the island, one dear son
Shall I twice lose.

Ferdinand – now freed from Prospero's magic – speaks for himself for the first time.

FERDINAND:
Though the seas threaten, they are merciful;
I have cursed them without cause.
ALONSO:
Now all the blessings
Of a glad father compass thee about!
Arise, and say how thou cam'st here.

Miranda – freed from the influence of her father's manipulations –– speaks for the first time.

MIRANDA:
O, wonder!
How many goodly creatures are there here!
How beauteous mankind is! O brave new world,
That has such people in't!
PROSPERO:
'Tis new to thee.

ALONSO:
What is this maid with whom thou wast at play?
Your eld'st acquaintance cannot be three hours:
Is she the goddess that hath severed us,
And brought us thus together?
FERDINAND:
Sir, she is mortal;
But, by immortal Providence, she's mine:
I chose her when I could not ask my father
For his advice, nor thought I had one. She
Is daughter to this famous Duke of Milan,
Of whom so often I have heard renown,
But never saw before; of whom I have
Received a second life; and second father
This lady makes him to me.
ALONSO:
I am hers:
But, O, how oddly will it sound that I
Must ask my child forgiveness!
PROSPERO:
There, sir, stop:
Let us not burthen our remembrance with
A heaviness that's gone.
GONZALO:
I have inly wept,
Or should have spoke ere this. Look down, you gods,
And on this couple drop a blessed crown!
For it is you that have chalked forth the way
Which brought us hither.
ALONSO:
I say Amen, Gonzalo!
GONZALO:
Was Milan thrust from Milan, that his issue
Should become Kings of Naples? O, rejoice
Beyond a common joy! and set it down
With gold on lasting pillars: in one voyage
Did Claribel her husband find at Tunis,
And Ferdinand, her brother, found a wife
Where he himself was lost, Prospero his dukedom
In a poor isle, and all of us ourselves
When no man was his own.
ALONSO (to Ferdinand and Miranda):
Let grief and sorrow still embrace his heart
That doth not wish you joy!

GONZALO:
Be it so! Amen!

The crew of Alonso's ship enter.

GONZALO:
I prophesied, if a gallows were on land,
This fellow could not drown. What is the news?
BOATSWAIN (speaking for the first time):
The best news is, that we have safely found
Our King, and company; the next, our ship –
Which, but three glasses since, we gave out split –
Is tight and yare and bravely rigged, as when
We first put out to sea.

Enter Ariel, Caliban, Stephano and Trinculo.

STEPHANO (speaking for the first time):
Every man shift for all the rest, and let no man take care
for himself; for all is but fortune.
TRINCULO (speaking for the first time):
If these be true spies which I wear in my head, here's a
goodly sight.
CALIBAN speaking for the first time):
O Setebos, these be brave spirits indeed!
How fine my master is! I am afraid
He will chastise me.
SEBASTIAN:
What things are these, my lord Antonio?
Will money buy 'em?
ANTONIO (speaking for the first time):
Very like; one of them
Is a plain fish, and, no doubt, marketable.
PROSPERO:
Mark but the badges of these men, my lords,
Then say if they be true. This mis-shapen knave,
His mother was a witch; and one so strong
That could control the moon, make flows and ebbs,
And deal in her command, without her power.
These three have robbed me; and this demi-devil –
For he's a bastard one – had plotted with them
To take my life. Two of these fellows you
Must know and own; this thing of darkness I
Acknowledge mine.
CALIBAN:
I shall be pinched to death.

PROSPERO (to Caliban):
Go, sirrah, to my cell;
Take with you your companions; as you look
To have my pardon, trim it handsomely.

They walk forward and the spirits – the mythological host – encourage them to enter the now greatly
expanded doors of the porticoed entry into the
great pyramid – where inside – a great banquet is
being prepared.

PROSPERO:
Sir, I invite your Highness and your train
To my poor cell, where you shall take your rest
For this one night; and in the morn
I'll bring you to your ship, and so to Naples,
Where I have hope to see the nuptial
Of these our dear-beloved solemnised;
And thence retire me to my Milan, where
Every third thought shall be my grave.
I'll promise you calm seas, auspicious gales,
And sail so expeditious, that shall catch
Your royal fleet far off.

Ariel, hovering in the orange-trees by Prospero's
head, speaks for the first time.

ARIEL:
Sir, all this service have I done since I went.
Was't well done?

159

PROSPERO:
Bravely, my diligence. Thou shalt be free.

Ariel disappears.

89.15   Prospero shows his guests into a great banqueting hall. The camera moves forward with the guests and we are introduced to the feast. The camera and Prospero stop on the threshold of the hall.

It is a banquet of Veronese proportions . . . servant-spirits in a recognisable livery – maybe with whitened and rouged faces – serve unlimited food. There is music . . . candles . . . fountains . . . dogs . . . monkeys . . . dwarfs . . . light on silk and bare flesh . . . dancers . . . acrobats . . . feathers . . . flowers . . . bouquets . . . towels . . . cushions . . . gilt chairs . . . mirrors . . . rose-petals . . . spilt wine and a growing noise of chattering and laughter – the Renaissance nobleman's idea of a good time.

We watch Alonso and his company escorted – through the throng – to their seats at table – Ferdinand and Miranda sitting in throne-like chairs . . . then the camera retreats back through a crowd of spirit-servants at the wide, imposing doors . . . around us . . . mythological creatures continue to carry in food and wine and presents.

As we retreat – coming – symmetrically in the exact centre of the picture – through the throng of guests and servants in the hall is the walking figure of Ariel – he is trundling a wheelbarrow . . . modest and businesslike – he arrives beside Prospero.

89.16   Close-up. In the barrow are books – Prospero's magic books – the ones he has decided to drown . . . all twenty-four of them . . . plus one more – the unfinished book of *The Tempest*.

89.17   Prospero turns away from the doors of the banqueting hall and sets off with Ariel – who, following on – pushes the barrow of books.

SECTION 90
ABOVE THE SEA

90.1   Prospero – in a blue version of his cloak . . . walks along a cliff-path – away from the revels and the noise of the banquet . . . away from the silhouette of the palaces against a bright starry sky with a crescent moon.

Prospero and Ariel are small silhouettes against the huge sweep of the night sky (a reminder of the Milanese night when Prospero was arrested).

SECTION 91
ON THE SEA'S EDGE

91.1   A travelling shot – the camera retreats before Prospero and Ariel who are both lit by the

glow of the books in the wheelbarrow. They walk along a strand towards the sea. The sounds of the banquet hall grow faint – losing volume under the sounds of the sea and the wind in the grass and a nocturnal seabird. Through these natural sounds, the mechanical droning noise that precedes Prospero's music is heard getting louder. Prospero's cloak begins to glow fire-red.

They arrive at a rocky outcrop twenty feet above the calm sea.

91.2 Taking the books from the wheelbarrow . . . Ariel passes them to Prospero – who briefly regards them – then . . . with gestures that are almost nonchalant . . . he hurls them into the sea . . .

91.3 Prospero holds (1) *The Book of Water* (Shot 1.2). In expectation of its destruction . . . it starts to liquefy before it is thrown. The print of the text smudging, the drawings blotting, the pages

becoming white and clean and empty.

91.4 It hits the water with a splash of white light and a thunder-clap and a scattering of white rain. Prospero's music starts with a great crash and the demise of the mechanical-magic noise.

91.5 Prospero picks up (2) *A Book of Mirrors* (Shot 10.2). Its mirrored pages flash reflections in his face. When he hurls it into the air over the cliff – it screams like a firework and hits the water with a magnesium-flare splash.

91.6 (3) *The Book of Mythologies* (Shot 14.4). Seen thrown from Prospero's hand – its pages flying loose as it leaves his hand and scattering – like a thousand white gulls – into the water.

91.7 (4) *A Primer of the Small Stars* (Shot 16.10). When it hits the water – it explodes, sending up a plume of white smoke.

91.8 (5) *An Atlas Belonging to Orpheus* (Shot

161

33.5). We see the book from underwater as it disintegrates, pluming inky black dye.

91.9 (6) *A Harsh Book of Geometry* (Shot 33.9). Reluctant to leave Prospero's hand, it bursts into green flame flying through the air.

91.10 (7) *The Book of Colours* (Shot 33.11). It hits the water and bursts open in a confusion of brilliantly-coloured dyes.

91.11 (8) *The Vesalius Anatomy of Birth* (Shot 34.1). As it hits the water, it screams and spurts blood like a pierced heart – as it sinks, there is a suggestion of entrails.

91.12 (9) *The Alphabetical Inventory of the Dead* (Shot 34.27). Seen on the sandy sea-bed, burying itself in the sand like a crab.

91.13 (10) *A Book of Travellers' Tales* (Shot 34.33). As it hits the water its pages detach themselves from the covers, which sink . . . and the pages form themselves into small paper boats that float away on the tide.

91.14 (11) *The Book of the Earth* (Shot 35.3). It floats on the sea boiling with acids, scalding water, hissing steam and bubbling foam.

91.15 (12) *A Book of Architecture and Other Music* (Shot 35.9). Underwater – the book falls swiftly through the water – trailing fragments of masonry, rubble and sand.

91.16 (13) *The Ninety-Two Conceits of the Minotaur* (Shot 43.14). The book reluctantly sinks in a mess of blood and bile and bubbles, leaving an oily slick.

91.17 (14) *The Book of Languages* (Shot 43.18). The book – at the moment of throwing – falls to pieces like a collection of bone-dry wafers – a brown dust blows away on the wind.

91.18 (15) *End-Plants* (Shot 44.2). It hits the water and refuses to sink – it becomes a raft of butterflies and dragonflies surrounded by floating flower-heads.

91.19 (16) *The Book of Love* (44.22). It flies through the air in a cloud of pink petals and hits the water with a splash of milk and blood.

91.20 (17) *A Bestiary of Past, Present and Future Animals* (47.2). Seen floating – above and below the water – a refuge for small animals – tadpoles, newts, small clinging fish, snails and limpets.

91.21 (18) *The Book of Utopias* (Shot 56.1). It falls through the water in a fizz of bubbles.

91.22 (19) *The Book of Universal Cosmography* (Shot 73.1). As it hits the water – it disappears, leaving a green stain, hissing steam and a swirl of phosphorescence.

91.23 (20) *Love of Ruins* (Shot 75.3). It falls and sinks like the block of stone it resembles.

91.24 (21) *The Autobiographies of Pasiphae and Semiramis* (80.1). It flies through the air in flames and hits the water bubbling with black pitch.

91.25 (22) *The Book of Motion* (Shot 82.3). Prospero undoes the straps that bind it and all its pages immediately break free – as though never bound – they blow away.

91.26 (23) *The Book of Games* (Shot 89.12). The book floats on the water surrounded by the hundreds of playing-pieces – draughts, pawns, chequers, knights etc.

91.27 Only two books are left – a thick volume called (24) *Thirty-Six Plays* . . . and – bound identically – but much slimmer – Prospero's unfinished (25) *The Tempest*. Turning both books slowly in his hands – we can see that on the spine of *Thirty-Six Plays* is the name William Shakespeare – opening the book we catch – as the pages turn – the many familiar names of Shakespearean plays – the text is written entirely by hand – Prospero's hand. Prospero makes a decision and throws them both into the sea.

91.28 The books land together on the water and Caliban surfaces – spurting and spouting water from a long underwater swim – he snatches both books and disappears again under the surface. The water is calm . . . as though it had never been a witness to the destruction of so many books.

91.29 The whole sequence has been accompanied by Prospero's magic music – orchestrating the destruction of the books. It now reaches a high point. Watched by Ariel, who now stands beside the empty wheelbarrow, Prospero takes his magic stick – the crozier-like wand – and snaps it in half. The music abruptly stops – there is a great silence

– we hear the wind, waves and noctural seabirds.

91.30 Here begins a montage. As Prospero's magic is nullified – so the products of that magic disappear. There are inevitable comparisons and deliberate correspondences between this breakdown and the former collapse of the masque. The wholesale disappearance and destruction is accompanied by 'natural' sound.

(1) The water in the bath-house bath (where the film began) – evaporates.

(2) A pile of books in the bath-colonnade topples over.

(3) The sleeping lion in the bath-house yawns and fades away.

(4) The banquet livery worn by a servant evaporates a second or so before the servant.

(5) Pages fall out of a book.

(6) Piled fruit in a dish in the banquet hall disappears a second before the dish.

(7) The columns of the palaces begin to crack.

(8) An inkwell topples, flooding books with black ink – ink and books fade, leaving a bare desk-top.

(9) The golden vines around the trees in the forest begin to slip.

(10) Text on a page disappears as though attacked by acid a second before the page itself disappears.

(11) Bacchanalian servants in the banquet hall fade away in the space of a gesture.

(12) The flowers in a maenad's hair disappear.

(13) Books in the library begin to fall off the shelves.

(14) Exotic plants begin to collapse as though now made of old paper.

(15) Oranges fall off orange-trees and fade before they hit the ground.

(16) Carved inscriptions on the pyramid fall away.

(17) A glass ewer falls from a table – but before we anticipate its smash – it evaporates.

(18) The palaces begin to sway and topple as in an earthquake – but as the columns keel and the architraves crack – they disappear . . . they evaporate . . .

(19) Wine being poured from a jug into a glass dries up.

(20) Grass grows white.

(21) The trees and vegetation and flora wither – they grow grey and white . . . become powdery – like old paper – they shrivel and contract and fade away.

(22) A herd of animals freeze in mid-gesture and fade away.

(23) More books in the library begin to fall and topple from the shelves – but they fade before they reach the floor.

(24) Alonso and his company look on astonished as the food before them disappears.

(25) A table-cloth begins to slip – dragging with it crockery and flowers – it disappears before it hits the floor.

(26) Alonso's fine clothes begin to wilt.

(27) A wind whips pages into the air before they vanish.

(28) Against the night sky – Alonso and company – sit on bare stools on a stretch of flat rock – their finery diminished.

91.31 Prospero – on the sea-cliff – hurls the two pieces of his wand into the sea.

91.32 On the surface of the sea – the two pieces of Prospero's wand turn into green sea-serpents and at once swim away.

91.33 There now begins the last shot of the film – a single, virtuoso, bravura take.

Prospero picks up Ariel and embraces and kisses him.

PROSPERO:
My Ariel, chick, to the elements
Be free, and fare thou well!

Prospero turns to camera and looks straight at us – the audience.

PROSPERO:
Please you, draw near.

The camera draws near, and he speaks to us intimately – on an individual one-to-one basis – his close-up face brightly lit against the void of the sky – a dignified mortal – not a god or a magician or a Duke or a King.

PROSPERO:

Now my charms are all o'erthrown,
And what strength I have's mine own –
Which is most faint: now, 'tis true,
I must be here confined by you,
Or sent to Naples. Let me not,
Since I have my dukedom got,
And pardoned the deceiver, dwell
In this bare island by your spell;
But release me from my bands
With the help of your good hands:
Gentle breath of yours my sails
Must fill, or else my project fails,
Which was to please.

Now Prospero/Shakespeare breaks the theatrical/
filmic illusion by appealing directly to his
audience . . . and all his audiences . . . and his last
audience in his last play . . . as he takes leave of the
island, the theatre and – possibly his life.
The camera retreats on his close-up to show that it
is – self-reflexedly – a close-up on a huge screen.
The naked Ariel has climbed up the back of the
screen and is now climbing over it – like a small
cherubic child scrambling over a wall . . . Ariel has
lost a little of his magic – maybe his curls are not so
pronounced . . . his body is whiter and less perfect
. . . he scrambles over the screen – now seen at a
slight angle and in slight perspective . . . and
adroitly drops swiftly to the ground in front of the
screen – across Prospero's face. Ariel's white body
contrasts with the black around Prospero's head
and with the empty velvet void around the screen
and on the ground.
Once on the ground, Ariel begins to run towards
the camera, which is retreating smoothly . . . leaving Prospero's talking head on screen – growing
smaller and smaller behind him. Prospero's voice
is still loud – whispering intimately in our ear.
Ariel now runs through crowds of courtiers –
males outnumber females – elegantly overdressed
in the style of Alonso's court. The courtiers watch
Ariel run past as they listen to Prospero's last
words.

PROSPERO:

Now I want
Spirits to enforce, Art to enchant;
And my ending is despair,
Unless I be relieved by prayer,
Which pierces so, that it assaults
Mercy itself, and frees all faults.
As you from crimes would pardoned be,
Let your indulgence set me free.

Prospero – still in close-up on the screen – bows
his head slightly, and then closes his eyes.
The increasing number of courtiers start to clap.
Prospero's distant close-up screen image continues to retreat as Ariel – approaching the camera
(which has let him catch up) now occupies most of
the screen-space. Ariel is now running faster to
gain speed to jump, launch himself and fly to freedom.
There are more and more courtiers clapping –
Ariel runs through and between them . . . a diminutive child-figure among tall adults . . . he gains
speed all the time.
When Ariel is very close to us . . . he suddenly – by
a trick . . . runs up and over our heads . . . up a slope
we cannot see . . . and into the sky . . . the camera
tips and swings 180 degrees to see Ariel jump in a
huge diving leap, as though about to jump from a
high diving-board.
Ariel arcs across the black sky as the camera
watches him . . . and he disappears into the black
sea/sky with an echoing splash – the showering
white-against-black water-droplets splash up high
in the air in slow-motion . . .
Ariel has gone and the returning splash-water falls
into black water . . .
A series of ever-decreasing splashes
drip and plop into black water . . .
thus the beginning of the film
is reprised.
A final splash plops . . . all
water-movement ceases
and the screen is a black
velvet void.

CAST LIST

PROSPERO	John Gielgud
CALIBAN	Michael Clark
ALONSO	Michel Blanc
GONZALO	Erland Josephson
MIRANDA	Isabelle Pasco
ANTONIO	Tom Bell
SEBASTIAN	Kenneth Cranham
FERDINAND	Mark Rylance
ADRIAN	Gerard Thoolen
FRANCISCO	Pierre Bokma
TRINCULO	Jim Van De Woude
STEPHANO	Michael Romeyn
ARIEL	Orpheo, Paul Russell, James Thierree and Emil Wolk
IRIS	Marie Angel
CERES	Ute Lemper
JUNO	Deborah Conway

DIRECTOR OF PHOTOGRAPHY	Sacha Vierny
PRODUCTION DESIGNERS	Ben Van Os & Jan Roelfs
MUSIC	Michael Nyman
PRODUCTION SOUND	Garth Marshall
INFOGRAPHY	Eve Ramboz
EDITOR	Marina Bodbijl
DUBBING EDITOR	Chris Wyatt
ASSOCIATE PRODUCERS	Masato Hara and Roland Wigman
EXECUTIVE PRODUCERS	Kees Kasander and Denis Wigman
CO-PRODUCERS	Philippe Carcassonne and Jean Louis Piel
PRODUCER	Kees Kasander
DIRECTOR	Peter Greenaway

FILM CREW

Production Manager: *Karin van de Werff*
Production Co-ordinators: *Brigitte Fauré (France) and*
Sophie Lambo (Holland)
1st Assistant Director: *Gerrit Martijn*
2nd Assistant Director: *Sophie Fiennes*
3rd Assistant Directors: *Edith Hazelebach and Paul Marbus*
Actors' Coach: *Milfid Ellis*

Location Manager: *Marty de Boer*
Assistant: *Rijk van den Berg*
Production Assistants: *Anja Cloosterman, Fulco Lorenzo, Bert Nijdam*
and Anke Battem
Accountant: *Boudewijn van der Donk*
Assistant Accountant: *Annelies Meuleman*
Runners: *Richard van Grinsven, Lars Kespel and Robert Streefland*

Camera Operator: *Chris Renson*
Focus Puller: *Valerie Dupin*
Continuity: *Anne van Aaken*
Clapper Loader: *Benito Strangio*
Chief Grip: *Martin McCullough*
Grip: *Bob Howland*
Assistant Grip: *Eric Schut*

Gaffer: *Reinier van Brummelen*
Electricians: *Pieter Vermeer, Dirk Nijland, Wouter Poppink and*
Pelle Herfst
Best Boy: *Nico Komen*
Boom Operators: *Mark Glynne and Paula Odino*

Assistant Art Directors: *Michael Howells and Ank van Straalen*
Art Department Production: *Eljo Embregts and Wilma Schuemie*
Set Dresser: *Constance de Vos*
Props: *Floris Vos*
Calligraphy: *Brody Neuenschwander*
Book Design: *Han Ing Lim, Agnes Charlemagne and Ellen Vomberg*
Book Design and Grasswork: *Daniel Harvey*

Construction Manager: *Wilbert van Dorp (SBI)*
Constructors: *Lidewij Kaptein (SBI), Dory van Noort (SBI) and*
Maarten Piersma
Assistant Constructors: *Hans Froger, Ruud van Vorstenbosch, Andre*
Peperkamp, David Peters, Rob Duiker, Dennis Los, Bas Boone and John
Rawsthorn

Decorators: *Ben Zuydwijk, Rick Overberg and Wendy Valentijn*
Assistant Decorator: *Claudia Valentijn*
Assistant Set Dressers: *Rayke Verhoeven, Jorien Sont and John Bramble*
Decor Assistants: *Selene Kolman, Linda Termans and Lilian Wadilie*
Driver: *Ron van de Woude*

Wardrobe Mistress: *Dien van Straalen*
Wardrobe Assistant: *Cynthia Roosberg*
Prospero's Creatures: *Ellen Lens*
Wardrobe Assistant: *Debbie Luiten*

Dresser for John Gielgud: *Mendel de Boer*
Stand-in for John Gielgud: *Jasper van der Linden*
Milanese Ruffs: *Maggie McMahon*
Milanese Hats: *Jacques Janssen*
Prospero's Cloak: *Emi Wada*
Assistant to Emi Wada: *Kayo Sakurai*

Hair and Make Up: *Sara Meerman*
Make Up Assistant: *Hanneke van Rhoon*
FX Make Up: *Sjoerd Didden*
Make Up Department: *Brigitte Pleizier, Anniek Widdershoven,*
Mariël Hoevenaars, Gaby van der Meijden and Petra van Harte

Dancers Choreography: *Karine Saporta*
Assistant to Karine Saporta: *Claire Magnenat*
Dancers: *Mirale Jusid, Helene Zellweger, Helene Busnel and*
Florence Gielen
Acrobatic Advisors: *Martine Le Roy and Stéphane Dupre*
Caliban Choreography: *Michael Clark*

Casting UK: *Karen Lindsay Stewart and Polly Hootkins*
Extras Casting: *FTV, Rotterdam*
Publicity: *Charles McDonald and Carlie Janszen (Allarts)*
Stills: *Marc Guillaumot*
Catering: *Tom Bergman and Marion Hunink*
Travel: *Italian Travel (London) and Foreign Affairs (The Hague)*

Music performed by *The Michael Nyman Band*
Ariel's songs sung by *Sarah Leonard*

Recorded and Mixed at *PRT Studios and Abbey Road Studios*
Music Producer: *David Cunningham*
Engineer: *Michael J Dutton*
Assistant Engineers: *Dillon Gallagher (PRT) and Chris Brown*
(Abbey Road)

 Michael Nyman's music for *Prospero's Books*
is available on Decca Records (London Records
in Nth and Sth America, Japan)

First Assistant Editor: *James Marshall*
Assistant Editors: *Loes Gisolf and Maxine Matts*
Digital Sound Editing: *Nigel Heath*
Dialogue Editor: *Shirley Shaw*
Dubbing Mixer: *Brian Saunders C.A.S.*
Re-recording Mixer: *Edward Colyer*
Footsteps Artists: *Jackie Austin and Anneli Daniell*
Book Narrator: *Leonard Maguire*
Sound Transfers: *Hackenbacker*
Re-recorded at: *Delta Sound Services*
Harry Facilities: *Mikros Image*
Opticals: *Image Creations*
Titles: *Frameline*
Processing: *Cineco Laboratories (Amsterdam) and Imagica (Japan)*

Camera supplied by *Camera Rentals (Amsterdam)*
Lights supplied by *Singelfilm (Amsterdam)*
Filmstock: *Kodak Netherlands*

NHK Hi-Vision Producers: *Yoshinobu Numano and Katsufumi Nakamura*
Assistant Producer: *Mitsuhiro Higashiyama*
NHK Hi-Vision Technical Supervisor: *Hideichi Tamegaya*
Technical Director: *Masao Yamaguchi*
Engineers: *Toshio Yamauchi and Toshiyuki Iino*
Telecine Engineers: *Noboru Michizoe and Toshio Tsunoda*
Production Co-ordinator: *Kayo Yoshida (Herald Ace, Inc)*
Assistant to Kayo Yoshida: *Utako Niimi*

With special thanks to: ASACA Corporation, Alexander Gelderman, Billy Hinshelwood, Ronnie Gerschtanowitz, Leo Mulder, Marc Thelosen, Ron Sterk, Victoria Chaplin and Jean Baptiste Thierrée, David Gothard, Holland Diving, Lissa Pillu, Romeo Gigli, Eileen Thomas, Liz de Jong, Dicky Parlevliet, Jean Louis Piel, Andi Wright, Museum Boymans-Van Beuningen (Rotterdam), Maritime Museum Prins Hendrik (Rotterdam), Museum Meermanno Westreenianum (The Hague), The Royal Library (The Hague), Teylers Museum (Haarlem), and the State Museum of Antiquites Leiden.

AN ANGLO-FRENCH CO-PRODUCTION
This film was made with the financial support of Eurimages Fund – of the council of Europe
Stichting Produktiefonds voor Nederlandse Films – and Pierson Heldring & Pierson Amsterdam

an ALLARTS – CINE/CAMERA ONE – PENTA co-production

PICTURE CREDITS

Drawings by Peter Greenaway.
Calligraphy by Brody Neuenschwander
Photographs by Marc Guillaumot pages 60, 63, 68, 95, 119, 140
Jacques Prayer/Gamma 1990 pages 41, 55, 129, 130, 132, 138, 142, 144, 157
Pief Weyman pages 46, 110/111

Acknowledgement is gratefully given for the following: 3, detail from a drawing of the Portuguese Fleet of Pedro Alvares Cabral in O Successo dos Visoreis by Lizuarte de Abreu (The Pierpont Morgan Library, New York, ref. M.525, f.16v-17); 38, Water falling into a pool by Leonardo da Vinci (Windsor Castle, The Royal Library. © 1991 Her Majesty The Queen); 40, St Jerome by Georges de la Tour (The National Museum, Stockholm); 42, detail from a Group of Ornamental Stairs Leading to a Rotonda by Giovanni Battista Piranesi (The Courtauld Institute of Art); 43, An Allegory with Venus and Cupid by Agnolo Bronzino (The National Gallery, London); 50, St Jerome in his Study by Antonello da Messina (The National Gallery, London); 59, the Atrium of the Laurenziana Library by Michelangelo Buonarroti (Biblioteca Medicea Laurenziana, Florence); 61, detail from The Birth of Venus by Sandro Botticelli (The Uffizi Gallery, Florence); 66 Above, A cheife Herowans wyfe of Pomeoc and her daughter . . . by John White (Trustees of the British Museum); 66 Below, A Cheiff Ladye of Pomeiooc, from *America* by Theodor de Bry (British Library); 67, Wedding Feast at Cana by Paolo Veronese (The Louvre, Paris); 70, title page of the first edition of *De Humanis Corporis Fabrica*, by Andreas Vesalius; 83, Pornocrates by Félicien Rops; 91, detail from Primavera by Sandro Botticelli (The Uffizi Gallery, Florence); 98, The Pyramids of Memphis from *Sphinx Mystagoga* by Athanasius Kircher (British Library); 99, detail from The Harvesters by Pieter Breughel (The Metropolitan Museum of Art, New York); 103, Bacchus and Ariadne by Titian (The National Gallery, London); 108, Portrait of Maerten Soolmans by Rembrandt van Ryn (Private collection; photograph from the Rijksmuseum, Amsterdam); 123, from *Tomus Secundus de Supernaturali, Naturali, Praeternaturali et Contranaturali Microcosmi historia*, by Robert Fludd; 141, The Doge Leonardo Loredan by Giovanni Bellini (The National Gallery, London); 152, The Ancient of Days by William Blake (Fitzwilliam Museum, Cambridge)

168